REMIX

REMIX

DECORATING WITH
CULTURE, OBJECTS, AND SOUL

Jeanine Hays & Bryan Mason

PHOTOGRAPHS BY PATRICK CLINE

Foreword by Danielle Colding,
host of HGTV's *Shop This Room*

POTTER STYLE
NEW YORK

Published in the United States by Potter Style, an imprint of
the Crown Publishing Group, a division of Random House, Inc., New York.
www.crownpublishing.com
www.potterstyle.com

POTTER STYLE is a trademark and POTTER with colophon
is a registered trademark of Random House, Inc.

Library of Congress Cataloging-in-Publication Data
Hays, Jeanine.
    Remix : decorating with culture, objects, and soul / Jeanine Hays and Bryan
Mason.—First Edition.
        pages cm
    Includes index.
    1. Interior decoration—United States.   2. African Americans—Homes and
haunts.   I. Mason, Bryan.   II. Title.
    NK2115.3.A47H39 2013
    747.089'96073—dc23   2012038317

ISBN 978-0-7704-3302-4
eISBN 978-0-7704-3303-1

Printed in China
Book and cover design by Ashley Tucker
Cover photograph by Patrick Cline

10 9 8 7 6 5 4 3 2 1

First Edition

TO OUR FAMILY, OUR FRIENDS,
AND EVERYONE OUT THERE
WITH **MODERN**, **SOULFUL STYLE**.

CONTENTS

FOREWORD

The first time I read Jeanine and Bryan's blog, *AphroChic,* I remember thinking to myself "Finally!"

Someone was finally starting a conversation about the influence of culture on design in a way that spoke to my experience. Someone was illustrating how to marry cultural influences with modern design in subtle, yet profound ways. I loved that *AphroChic* revealed how to tastefully incorporate global elements—textiles, patterns, wallpapers, art, and accessories—into contemporary interiors where clean lines and elegant details reign supreme. Best of all, these two bloggers were developing fresh interpretations of cultural patterns for wallpaper and fabrics that I could bring into my own home. Finally, a design conversation for someone like me!

As a multiracial woman born in the '70s in New York City, one of the most diverse cities in the world, I've never known anything other than a multicultural experience. From the food I ate to the music I listened to and the ethnic makeup within my own family members, my life experience has always been colored by myriad cultures, styles, and flavors.

My family's turn-of-the-century Tudor-style home was all about the mix, too, and

my mother was the queen mixologist. What is now a deliberate design style in most homes was then a practical necessity for us. As a single working mother, my mom had to make her money work for her. She blended styles because it made economical sense, and she perfected the art of it. An exquisite hand-carved lion table she bought after saving for months mingled with marble-topped and iron accent tables passed down from her father, a design aficionado. Sleek white-linen sofas and shag rugs paired with carvings bought on her honeymoon cruise to Haiti. For my mother, good design was all about surrounding herself with beautiful things that held personal meaning, and she found a place for everything she loved in our home. This education on eclecticism and exposure to a range of cultures set the stage for my own meandering path, from my studies in anthropology and modern dance to my career as an interior designer.

After I won *Design Star* on HGTV, Jeanine Hays was one of the first people to reach out to me and ask about my experience on the show. She was also the first to inquire about my anthropology background and how culture impacts my design approach. Her questions were insightful and grounded—she wanted a deeper understanding of my design style. I immediately knew I had met a kindred spirit. Since then I have had a chance to spend more time with Jeanine and the other half of *AphroChic*, her husband, Bryan. Jeanine's infectious smile and optimistic attitude and Bryan's love of intellectual debate and discussion hooked me right away. Our first meeting was akin to reuniting with old friends: we talked about design, politics, and food as if from one mind.

Now, through Jeanine and Bryan's labor of love, they have written *Remix*, a comprehensive guide to bringing a sense of cultural identity into the home while still honoring a modern design aesthetic. They show you how to add soulful flavor to interior spaces by paying homage to a diverse range of personal and cultural experiences.

This book is right on time. It reflects our increasingly global, multicultural, and multiethnic world, and encourages you to express yourself through a unique approach to design. *Remix* speaks to our commonalities, not our differences; at every corner, it seeks to include not divide. Most important,

this book is not only for people of African and African American descent. It is for anyone who loves decorating with exotic textiles, bold colors, or handcrafted furnishings and art.

What amazes me most about the design process Jeanine and Bryan describe is that it reflects who we are as people and how we really live our lives. Design is no longer a rarefied endeavor focused on amassing beautiful objects according to some archaic set of rules, nor does it require you to follow the latest trends. More than ever, designing a beautiful home is an opportunity for us to embrace our own unique backgrounds, experiences, and perspectives, and to manifest that individuality in our interiors. We have thrown out the idea of matching bedroom sets, loveseat and sofa combos, and an attachment to perfectionism. We want spaces that move us. More specifically, we want our spaces to reflect our best selves. And in *Remix* Jeanine and Bryan show us how.

—DANIELLE COLDING,
host of HGTV's *Shop This Room*

REMIX:
FROM AFROCENTRIC
TO APHROCHIC

We encourage every-
one to look at design
through their own
cultural lens in order to
decorate a home that
reflects who they are.

Over the past thirty years, *remix* has become a household word in African American music. The idea of a remix is simple: rearrange old songs by adding modern elements that give them new life. We can't think of a better way to describe our approach to modern design.

When we started our blog, *AphroChic,* our goal was to create a space that celebrated diversity and to showcase modern homes that have a unique cultural identity. As African Americans, our culture and heritage have always informed our design process, whether as inspiration for a new interpretation of an ancient textile or in choosing a bright color to paint our bedroom. At *AphroChic,* we believe that the relationship between culture and design holds importance for everyone, and we encourage everyone to look at design through their own cultural lens in order to decorate a home that reflects who they are. But keeping a space modern in today's global community means considering more than your own heritage. It also entails looking at the cultures that inspire you and finding meaningful ways to make them a part of your home's "story."

Over the years we have written about rugs inspired by the beauty of Morocco, pillows made by Indian artisans, and fashion illustrations featuring African American women—all perfect ways to bring soul and style to the modern white boxes so many of us live in. As we expanded from blogging to textile design, we realized people began wondering what this "Aphro" concept was all about.

AphroChic is a "remix," a subtle blending of modern and cultural influences that evokes rather than displays a cultural motif.

Ethnic culture and modern design are not mutually exclusive ideas. In fact, they are even better together.

AphroChic draws not only from traditional but also from recent African art and design. It reaches beyond familiar African influences to include the various cultures that have evolved within the African Diaspora—from the Caribbean and the Americas to Europe and Asia as well.

Our design philosophy embraces a global aesthetic. In an AphroChic room, African Kuba prints sit beside French toile while India-inspired mandala patterns adorn table

runners and Cameroonian juju hats decorate walls. We love the beauty of the global mix and have even brought it to our own textile collection, where so many ideas of pattern and global design intersect.

After years of growing, reflecting, and learning, we are now able to offer this book, which expands upon those concepts that first inspired our blog and our textile line. We believe that ethnic culture and modern design are not mutually exclusive ideas. In fact, we know that they are even better together. This book gives you design principles for bringing your personality, heritage, and love of styles from around the world into your

ABOVE: Color, pattern, art, and global objects bring this living room to life. **OPPOSITE, LEFT:** Display cultural pieces with a contemporary aesthetic, like this modern African American painting. **OPPOSITE, RIGHT:** Add color with an Eames chair. **PREVIOUS PAGE:** Bring color and pattern home with textiles and unexpected decorative objects.

THIS PAGE: In a Manhattan home, ikat cushions add cultural style to Lucite chairs and a chrome dining table. OPPOSITE: In our home, we decorate with beautiful culturally inspired textiles that we produce, from modern Kuba prints to African American–inspired patterns.

own home—today, and even decades from now. AphroChic does not treat culture as a trend. Instead, we built our design philosophy around a deep, sophisticated, and authentic engagement with cultures that have lasted long beyond trends.

In order to show off exciting examples of AphroChic style, we traveled to homes in some of our favorite cities: New York, Los Angeles, Philadelphia, and Washington, DC. Patrick Cline, cofounder of *Lonny* magazine, brought his own uniquely soulful vision to our project, shooting with film, a rare treat in this age of digital photography.

Color, pattern, original art, and global pieces are keys to bringing culture home.

Part One of this book, Elements, explores the basic principles that guide our own design process. With every piece we design, we spend time thinking about its color and pattern, the artistry that goes into its creation, and the global culture that inspires it. These very same design elements—color, pattern, original art, and global pieces—are the keys to bringing culture home and have played a major role in the style of every home that appears in this book.

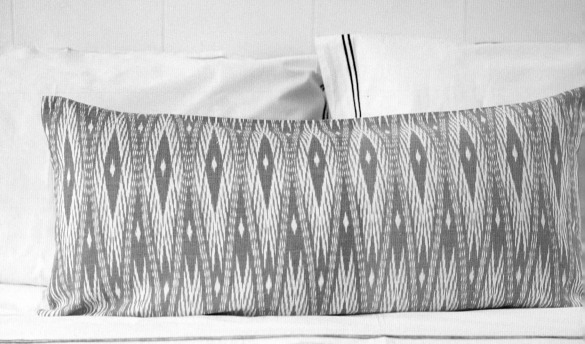

In Part Two, Modern Soulful Homes, we take you into the spaces of people who have successfully brought together all four design elements, creating homes layered with meaning, history, and heritage, mixed with modern flair. Each homeowner has a fascinating story behind the design of their space, and each house tour ends with a quick recap of the decorative details that make these homes distinct and memorable, so you can learn how to create a space that shows off your soulful side. At the end of this book, we have curated a selection of our favorite resources—including museums, artisans, and designers—so you'll know just where to look for modern, soulful style.

Our dream is that years from now, you will be able to look back at these pages and still discover new ways to blend modern and cultural details for a home that evokes soulfulness. We hope that this book inspires you to build a sophisticated and authentic style that is truly AphroChic.

A single piece can speak to several of the elements presented in this book. A traditional ikat represents a cultural pattern with a centuries-old history. In bold tangerine, it is also a colorful statement piece.

CLOCKWISE FROM TOP LEFT:
Simple elements, like hot-pink storage bins can be used to create a vibrant display on IKEA's popular Expedit shelving unit. Cultural objects can come in the form of accessories or hand-carved furnishings like this beautiful wooden chair. A shimmering bust encrusted in silver tiles is an unconventional yet fascinating sculpture in a homeowner's unique art collection.

PART ONE

ELEMENTS

Color | Pattern | Art | Global Objects

The building blocks of every room are the gateway to bringing emotion, culture, your personal story, and the rest of the world into your home. Explore the elements of AphroChic style and learn how to use them to transform your space into a true reflection of who you are.

1
THE
CULTURE
OF
COLOR

In many African American homes, color comes first. The use of bright shades and warm tones seemed to be everywhere

when we were growing up. Whether we were spending time with our grandparents, our cousins, or even in our own childhood homes, color made its way into our lives through furnishings, paint treatments, and pieces handed down from generation to generation. Bright colors were everywhere, and they continue to shape the way that we view interiors.

While many designers think of color as way to set the tone and even add a wow factor to a room, we like to think of it as the first cultural accent piece in your home. For our AphroChic textile line, the design begins with our thoughts on color and pattern. With a bold shade we can immediately update a cultural pattern or a traditional motif that inspires us, remaking it into something new and relevant for today's interiors.

Color can complement many antique or globally inspired pieces that accent your home. Whether it's an accessory, like a pillow with an African-inspired print, or a wallpaper pattern with a retro design, opt for cultural pieces in fresh color combinations for a modern update on traditional, global motifs. Color can be a nod to cultural heritage and to the unique story that you want to tell in your interior.

Discovering Your Perfect Shade

As designers, choosing the right color palette for our work comes down to a number of factors. For months in advance, we research color choices for a specific season, reviewing Pantone swatches and trend reports for the right shades for our accessories. But in decorating our own home, we choose tones that have a particular meaning to us.

OPPOSITE: Warhol's *Queen Ntombi Twala* is the inspiration for this dining nook's color palette.
PREVIOUS PAGE: A jewel-tone rug, colorful side chairs, and painted architectural details are used to make a colorful statement in this home.

Colors can set the stage for a feminine space. In this bedroom, vivid shades create a whimsical touch. A settee upholstered in turquoise velvet is the pop that brings this girly space to life.

To discover the perfect color palette for your interior, it's important to ask yourself a few key questions that will get you on the right path to bold, beautiful, and cultural color:

WHAT DOES COLOR MEAN TO ME?

Color can be a strong reminder of a homeland, an ethnic heritage, or even a childhood memory. Teal walls can evoke clear skies over a midwestern plain or act as a tribute to a Caribbean ancestry. Pink, a color that Jeanine loves to include in her interiors, never fails to remind her of the first room that she designed at age six in a pink-and-red palette inspired by her favorite doll, Strawberry Shortcake. We live our lives with color. And for each of us there are colors that remind us of our favorite moments from the past. These shades lend a deep and personal meaning to our spaces, making them feel more comfortable. Once you've figured out which hues speak to you, you can develop a color palette that will always score a smile.

ABOVE LEFT: This painting injects a smile-inducing color into this space, adding an element of fun to this traditional room.
ABOVE RIGHT: An apple-red Chinese cabinet brings color and culture together in this bedroom.

WHAT EMOTION WILL COLOR BRING TO MY SPACE?

Think about how a particular color makes you feel. A calm and soothing shade may conjure up happy memories, but it might not be the most motivating color to bring into a home office, where you may want to spark your creativity and productivity. Ask yourself: What do I want this room to do for me? Should the design be bold and invigorating, or cool and calming, or something else altogether? The power of color can make you feel energized or peaceful. It can make you feel nostalgic or giddy. It can even make you feel optimistic and alive. It can center you on where you are or lift your spirits and take you far, far away. Figuring out how you want your room to make you feel will help you to identify the hues that will be the starting point for your perfect space.

WHAT STORY AM I TRYING TO TELL?

Essentially your home is the story of you. Every room has the ability to convey your travels, your history, and even your ancestry. No matter what story you're trying to tell, color can set the stage. Will your room speak to your travels to Morocco? Perhaps

The right colors can tell a complete story. Soothing accents like beige, teal, coral, and green transform a backyard pool into a Mediterranean Moroccan paradise with colors that evoke a perfect day at a Mediterranean beach.

you'll decide to mix in a few bits of gold and silver to create the sense of extravagance and mystery that you found in Marrakesh. Whether your design tells where you've been, where you are, or where you want to go, color can be your first step on that journey.

Soulful Hues We Love

When telling a story through color, the key is to know what shades will create your desired effect. Color is inherently emotional, and so in addition to using it to bring in culture, you can also use it as a way to establish the emotional content of the room. Whether you're trying to create a warm, energetic, or soothing effect in your room, it helps to know which colors can create that perfect feeling. And while some shades may come and go out of fashion, the feelings that they bring will last much longer.

ENERGIZING SHADES

When Michelle Obama wore a **mimosa yellow** coat to the presidential inauguration in 2009, the golden hue became an instant classic. The color is energizing, sunny, and a feel-good shade that will make you smile.

The ultimate power color, **red** is an iconic cultural shade. It can be found on every continent from Africa to Asia and is a powerful hue in fashion as well as home décor. Just a few red details go a long way, like a throw blanket on a bed or a red cushion. Red can add a powerful boost to rooms painted in navy blue, black, and even green, its complementary shade.

Girly, bright, and a little bit funky, **fuchsia** is another feel-good shade that can be even more invigorating than red when injected into a space at the right moments. It doesn't take much to create a big impact with fuchsia. Mix it with deep dark browns for a sophisticated look, or try it next to saffron yellow for a retro vibe.

CLOCKWISE FROM TOP LEFT: Just like mimosa yellow, citron green is an energizing shade in a room that sparkles with glass. A Tivoli radio packs the perfect punch of vibrant red. Bright hues like tangerine can be splashed throughout in the form of small accessories or even a bouquet of flowers. A Chippendale chair gets a girly makeover with a bright fuchsia cushion.

Rich, spicy, warm, and energizing, **tangerine** looks good on absolutely anything, from walls to furniture to accessories. It can be mixed with a variety of diverse colors, from bright fuchsia to pastel shades like mint. The juicy orange tone is sure to enliven any room in your space.

CALM AND SOOTHING COLORS

The color of the sea, **turquoise** evokes peace and tranquility, and for those whose family history includes a life by the water, it can transport them to their ancestral home. It's the perfect color to get lost in and just float way.

Peaceful and calming, pale **lavender** makes everything around it more beautiful. It's gorgeous on the walls and is clean and sophisticated when paired with neutral tones of brown, gray, and even black.

A blushing orange tone, **coral** is both warm and soothing at the same time. It looks fresh and modern against stark white and can be glammed up with splashes of gold and copper.

WARM NEUTRALS

We love wood tones. Natural and earthy **browns** in shades of honey and walnut brown can add depth to a room. Use hand-carved furniture to bring in these earthy shades, especially pieces that showcase the deep color of wood grain, from light to dark brown.

The color of midnight, **black** can be intimidating, but it can be that hue that brings bold, sexy, and glamorous style to your home. This shade is the perfect backdrop for jewel tones like emerald green, teal, yellow, and purple, which all come to life when set against a black background. And when paired with gold, black is warm and luxurious.

We love those special, warm tones of **white**, like cream, off-white, and those with just a hint of brown. White is a great backdrop that can be warmed up with wood and brighter tones to make a space feel both open and spacious.

Each of these colors can define a room in a million different ways. Paint, furniture, and accessories are all tools you can use to show off your room's color palette and contribute to the overall effect of the colors you choose. Whatever way you want to use color, go beyond trends and make sure that the color is meaningful to the story you are telling in your home.

ABOVE: Renew an antique piece in one of your favorite colors. Here, a dresser painted in coral feels fresh and modern. **LEFT:** Pair earthy browns with metallic shades for a glamorous look. Here, a silver, gold, and copper sculpture accentuates a wooden credenza. **OPPOSITE, LEFT:** Add color with a beautiful antique rug, like this ABC Carpet & Home Color Reform Rug in Turquoise. **OPPOSITE, RIGHT:** Warm gray tones, like the ones in this Kelly Wearstler pillow, can layer color onto a neutral backdrop.

Black Is Beautiful

Rooms that embrace dark, moody hues are so appealing. Black is a dramatic color to put on your walls and has the power to change a room in so many different ways. But with all our talk about bright and bold colors, you're probably asking: why go black?

In many modern interiors, white is considered the ideal neutral backdrop for colorful furnishings and accessories, yet black can provide as strong a foundation as white. Black walls can work in a space the same way that white walls do—just in a different way. Instead of a neutral base, black creates a dramatic backdrop for showcasing your favorite shades. When paired with bright jewel tones for furnishings and accessories, black sends colorful pieces to the forefront, and what could be more beautiful than that? Think about these tips when using black in your home:

- The other hues in a room really stand out against the black walls and dark flooring. Bring brightly colored furniture, accent chairs, and accessories like pillows and poufs into a black room. The juxtaposition of light and dark can turn a room into a celebration of eye-popping shades.

- Black can be a great backdrop for original art. Think bold abstract paintings with gold-toned frames that will really pop against a dark wall.

- When you're looking for a little glamour, mix black with metallic elements. Gold, silver, copper, and chrome sparkle against the dark hue. With a mix of metals, the room will look absolutely luxurious.

- For a classic look, pair black with white and wood tones. White trim or molding can make a room in black look sophisticated, and wood furnishings will warm up the dark color palette.

- For the perfect shade of black, try chalkboard paint. It's not too dark or saturated. And if you're not quite ready to commit to the darkest of shades, gray and navy blue can be used to create similar effects in a room without feeling overpowering.

Black patterned wallpaper can be used to create a striking feature wall. In this elegant home office, framed art, brass finishes, and a Lucite desk stand out against the cool black backdrop.

The color palette in this room has been set using one cultural piece—a South African pouf upholstered in an African batik fabric. Red, blue, and yellow all come into play in a palette built upon a beautiful piece of seating.

A Colorful Heritage

Recently, we visited one of the world's largest interior design trade shows, Maison & Objet in Paris. Walking the halls we were struck by how designers from around the world were utilizing color in furnishings and accessories. Outdoor mats from South Africa were woven with deep electric hues. Chinese teapots were reimagined in bright yellow and hot pink. And furniture was showcased in a variety of shades from deep orange to emerald green.

The trip was inspiring and proved to us that bright and vibrant shades not only keep with current home décor trends but can also express a cultural point of view.

A love of your own ancestral heritage and an appreciation for other cultures can both play an important part in choosing color for your home. Find shades that have cultural significance to you: reds can evoke an Asian feel; deep indigos can bring in an African vibe; and shades of turquoise and gold can be reminders of India. The right color choices are a critical step when turning an empty room into a statement of culture.

Online Color Inspiration

Just a few years ago, creating the perfect color palette was a long process of ordering samples, comparing swatches, clipping magazines, and creating mood boards to help make sense of it all. Now, creating a palette is as easy as clicking through a few links. We love using online resources to help us develop the perfect palette for our projects. Here are just a few:

PANTONE (PANTONE.COM) is the global authority on color. Designers view Pantone swatches and chips years in advance to help develop the right shades for their products. Visit the Pantone website for some amazing color inspiration. With the Pantone app, take photos of colors you want to use and get the color that best matches your snapshot.

RIGHT: Mood boards may have gone virtual, but you can still clip images out of your favorite design magazines and catalogs to create an inspiration board in your home. **OPPOSITE:** Take a cue from Pantone for color inspiration. The tangerine-orange accessories in this office were inspired by a Pantone Color of the Year.

PINTEREST (PINTEREST.COM) is a virtual mood board, allowing you to create collections of images, color swatches, and photos for a visual scrapbook. Pinterest boards are great tools for spotting themes in your design interests. Start by creating a board with a specific room in mind and simply pin inspiring images from your favorite online magazines and websites. As you bring these photos together, look for recurring colors that might serve as a starting point for a color palette. We started our own series of "Color Crush" boards for the *AphroChic* blog and it's been immensely helpful in sourcing inspiration for our own home and designs.

When purchasing a colorful accessory or shade of paint, you should definitely try the color first before going all the way. Paint sites like **BENJAMIN MOORE, VALSPAR,** and **OLYMPIC** allow you to order samples of paint before you buy an entire gallon. Just find a color or two that you like, order samples, and test them on the wall to see if any are right for you. It's that easy and worth the groundwork!

Layering Color

Implementing your color palette in an actual space can present a real challenge. While you may have identified a number of colors that you find meaningful and appealing, not every color you love needs to be represented in every room. So the question you'll find yourself asking is: how much color is too much?

Good design is often a matter of editing and deciding which colors should be dominant in your room and which ones should appear as accents. You may even have to ask yourself whether some of your favorite colors fit in at all. Maybe the bright yellow that you love is a bit too vibrant to use as the dominant color in a room that's meant to be laid-back and meditative. At the same time, white may seem like the perfect color to include in your living room, but bringing in an oversized white sofa may not be the right choice for a space where children will play. If you're looking for the perfect number of tones to define your room, remember that three isn't a crowd. In fact, it is the perfect number to help you layer colors in a way that is cohesive without making a space look too busy.

Layering colors can help create depth in your decorative scheme. Doing it well involves a subtle mixing and matching of the color in furniture, accessories, textiles, and art. A colorful mix can bring life to a space and make a home feel warm and lived-in, as if it's been curated over time. You can approach layering color in many different ways, but you just need to make a few choices to begin.

Once you have chosen a basic color palette of three or four colors for your space, the next step is to decide how to pull these shades together. Figuring out how to combine colors can be tricky. You can mull over color ratios and accents or spend hours looking at color wheels and charts. But, really, the decisions that you make can be as simple as choosing small, medium, and large uses of color.

chic tip Whenever you travel, find a cool shop and pick up a piece for your home in your favorite color. Not only are you creating an authentic collection of items that are memorable but you're also bringing in pieces that tell the story of where you've been and what you love.

THIS PAGE: The lush, glossy black wall in this bedroom is the perfect dramatic backdrop for a bright-red comforter and ikat print. **OPPOSITE:** The patterns and colors present in just one batik cushion can provide a great starting point for a room's color palette. Or keep it simple, like in this neutral bedroom, where one or two batik prints are all the color this space needs.

Blue flooring in the kitchen complements the bright color spectrum of red, orange, and yellow.

Large Color Choices

"Large" color choices are the ones that will define your room from the very beginning. Think of them as the colors you want to place on the main architectural details of your home—the walls, molding, floors, and built-ins like cabinetry and shelving. These are likely the most important color choices that you will make for your space. You might find yourself asking such questions as: What color should I paint the walls? Should I go with dark or light flooring? Should I go with white or black trim? Each of these decisions has an impact on the design of your home, and on how other colors are layered within. When deciding on the main colors for your space, consider the following:

Who said navy and black can't exist together? The homeowner chose to paint the walls dark blue as an alternative to painting the room black. The simple color palette comes together with contrasting pops of white and bright hues.

LEFT: This homeowner used ruby-red paint to accent built-in shelving in the kitchen and a growing collection of dishes for entertaining. **OPPOSITE:** Blue Plexiglas was used on the second floor of this home for a colorful transition between bedrooms. At night the glass lights up, turning the hallway light blue.

- Choose a wall color that will complement the furniture, art, and accessories. If you have a lot of art, crisp white walls may be a better backdrop for a rotating collection, rather than bold shades like purple or yellow, which might not complement each piece.

- Create colorful transitions in your home by staying in a color family and then varying the shade as a way to transition from room to room. That way, each space will have a distinctive and unique feel but still seem a part of the rest of the home.

- Don't forget about the ceiling. In large rooms with high ceilings, it can be fun to keep the eye moving all the way up with a ceiling shade that matches the entire room—or is even a shade or two lighter so that it doesn't feel heavy or oppressive.

- Accent built-ins with a colorful paint treatment, like painting the back wall of a bookshelf in a bold hue to make a stunning backdrop for the books and collections you have on display.

- Look for colorful flooring. You can envelop a room with bright tones by bringing the color palette all the way down to the floorboards. Wood that has been stained in shades of gray, purple, or blue can make a colorful statement and can even be a starting point for the colors you'll use on the wall.

- While in our own home we love white trim on the moldings for a classic look, you can bring in color and a graphic punch by outlining your room in an unexpected shade. How about black moldings or hot pink for shock value? Have fun playing with color and set your home apart from the rest.

Color is the star of this living room. A large white shelving unit comes to life with a pink paint treatment to accent books and keepsakes. A peacock-blue side chair is the accent piece that makes this room pop.

LEFT: This Hollywood Regency credenza steals the show as an accent piece painted kelly green and gold. **OPPOSITE:** A variety of medium color choices comes together in this living room with a gray sofa, black Kartell side table, and silver side table. With a neutral palette, smaller color choices like throw pillows can stand out.

Medium Color Choices

Once you have addressed the first layer of color, and your walls, floors, and built-ins are the perfect shade, it's time to decide on the color of your furnishings. Sofas, tables, and chairs all offer great opportunities to bring color into your room. When shopping for furniture, think of colorful pieces that can punctuate a space, or consider refinishing older pieces to give them new life. A bold furnishing can be the statement piece that makes the whole room, or it can be just one more accent in a home perfectly dotted with color throughout. Here are some great ideas for those "medium" color choices:

• These days, sofas are popping up in innovative colorways. Stores like Sofa.com let you customize sofas and chairs in luxe and colorful fabrics. We love the idea of a teal or bright yellow sofa in a living room.

• Colorful accent chairs have become an addiction in our own home. They are amazingly fun, and today you can find them in shades from neon yellows, to sumptuous reds and soft pastels.

- Modern dining chairs are another way to bring colorful seating home. Look at acrylic chairs from Knoll or Kartell. They come in a number of juicy colors, like Philippe Starck's "Ghost" chair, which is available in yellow, orange, green, and blue.

- Coffee tables in a range of colors can be an interesting way to add a pop of color to your living room. We recommend the IKEA "Lack" tables. They come in so many different colors that you can arrange two or even four together to create an unexpected mosaic.

- Keep an eye out for dining tables that go beyond the typical white, brown, and glass to make a colorful impression. To temper the color just a bit, surround the table with wooden chairs for contrast.

- Buffets, credenzas, and media carts can all steal the show when painted in eye-catching colors. CB2, West Elm, and Room & Board all have beautiful color-coated steel pieces.

CLOCKWISE FROM TOP LEFT:
Tabletop accessories, like glassware and coasters, are the perfect choice for colorful accent pieces in your home. Jonathan Adler's "Green Puzzle" pillow is a wonderful way to layer color into an otherwise neutral space. Even a small piece, such as a vase, can add just the right amount of color to any room. This hand-blown emerald-green vase makes a vivid statement among white and metallic pieces.

Small Color Choices

"Small" color choices are all about the accessories, the pieces that will finish and accentuate a room's color story. With your large and medium color choices anchoring the space, choosing the color of your accessories is where the real fun begins. Bring in bits of color through pieces like textiles, lighting, vases, and even picture frames. Best of all, these smaller pieces don't have to be a full-time commitment. Just swap them out whenever you want to introduce a new shade or style into your interior. Here are some tips for bringing in colorful accessories:

- With neutral furnishings like sofas and side chairs, add color with cushions and throws. Choose pillows in a few of your favorite shades, and then group them together for a splash of color in an otherwise neutral space.

- Use color in an unexpected way. Next time you entertain, create a tablescape with colorful dishes and flatware. Anthropologie latte bowls, which come in rainbow shades, including purple, green, coral, and blue, are our go-to pieces for adding bright elements to the dining room table.

- Make your travel souvenirs count. When traveling, find home accessories in your favorite shades, especially in colors that hold strong meaning for you. A gold vase from a visit to Paris or a red-and-white basket from your recent trip to South Africa can be the perfect way to tell your story through color.

- Use your DIY skills and turn a vintage piece or family heirloom into a colorful statement piece. Jeanine has a stool that she sat on as a child while watching her grandmother cook. She simply updated it by applying a fresh coat of paint to complement the color story in our home.

Color is the foundation of any home. No other design element has as much of an impact on how other elements will be introduced to a space or what they will do within the context of your overall cultural story. Whether it evokes the spirit of your ancestry or sets the emotional tone for your refuge from the stresses of everyday life, a wisely chosen and smartly blended color palette is key to creating a soulful space.

2
TELLING
YOUR STORY
THROUGH
PATTERN

Patterns hail from all over the world, many with long and interesting histories behind them. While color can allude to a feeling

or evoke a memory in your home, patterns have an even deeper connection to the places, people, and moments that created them. The right pattern can make a strong cultural statement that will set your interior apart from the rest by tapping into a history that may be centuries old. Currently popular designs like ikat, suzani, Kuba, and chevron all have ancient pasts that can tell a unique story in a modern way.

Pattern is the most obvious way for us to share our culture and heritage with the guests who enter our homes. But if used in an over-the-top way, it can be a bit overwhelming. For example, covering your walls and every piece of furniture in the same oversized pattern might not work. But layered together in small, understated bursts, patterns can add a sense of depth and sophistication to a room that few other décor elements can match. Moreover, the subtlety with which patterns signify a specific culture makes it possible to reference several cultures seamlessly within a single room. For example, a living room with a kanga cloth, a kasuri, and an antique kilim can speak to African cultures as well as Japanese and Turkish. Through pattern you can explore the world from your home and enjoy the richness of a space where all of your favorite cultures come together.

Traditional Patterns with a Modern Twist

Many of the patterns we explore in this chapter are very traditional. Some are centuries old, yet they still have an important place in modern design. But what makes these designs modern? The clean lines, minimalist style, and primary colors that are present in many of these patterns (or new interpreta-

PREVIOUS PAGE: Layer on a variety of patterns in a tight color palette for a striking mix. Here, ikat, floral, and chevron patterns come together in hues of blue, red, and white. **OPPOSITE:** Choose patterned pieces in modern colors, like this John Robshaw ikat pillow.

RIGHT: Use traditional patterns in new ways. Here, this hand-carved stool has been upholstered in a bright blue-and-white ikat pattern. While the pattern may be traditional, when used on a small stool it looks fresh and modern. **OPPOSITE:** The combination of stripes, polka dots, and various patterns is an extremely bold mix, but the variety of these patterns are toned down by a clean and simple color palette of black, white, and emerald green.

tions of these patterns) are all associated with modern design. Traditional patterns with traits that are popular today are an easy way to make an eye-catching statement that will break up a monochromatic or neutral space, giving it both a sense of identity and a unique touch. For patterned pieces to fit into your modern interior, look for time-honored designs that:

- APPEAR IN BOLD COLORS. Cultural patterns in contemporary shades feel current and updated.

- FEATURE GEOMETRIC LINES. Chevron and striped prints fit beautifully into modern interiors. The strong lines are a complement to the clean and straight elements that exist in modern spaces. When printed onto accessories, the pieces look like abstract works of art.

- HAVE A NEW INTERPRETATION. Many designers present traditional patterns and textile design in a new way to appeal to modern interiors. Look for designs that are traditional with a twist, like a blown-up, oversized design. Keep a look out for unique perspectives that will make your pattern stand apart.

Cultural Patterns and Textiles We Love

As the world becomes more closely connected through the web and social media, our ability to share designs and cultural aesthetics grows faster every day. As a result of that sharing, designers have made incredible efforts to reimagine classic and even ancient motifs from far-off places in modern colors and styles to make them feel fresh and relevant.

The following are our favorite cultural patterns that, with just a few updates, are finding new life in modern homes everywhere.

AFRICAN BATIKS

Though they are often associated with Southeast Asia, batik patterns also have a West African heritage. While it is difficult to say exactly when the technique emerged in African history, batik printing is a method widely used in West Africa. Designers form the patterns by applying pastes and wax to cotton before dying the fabric. The result is a blend of rich colors and intricate patterns created with natural materials and dyes. In today's interiors, these African wax prints have become beautiful accent pieces in the form of pillows, cushions, and poufs.

CHEVRONS

Simply an inverted V, chevrons continue to be among the most popular patterns in modern décor. The history of this design is long and varied; chevrons appear in many different places throughout much of human history. In Africa, the ruins of architecture featuring chevron patterns date from as far back as AD 1000, with Great Zimbabwe's eponymous "Houses of Stone" featuring the signature zigzag shape in its architecture. Even further back, chevron patterns have been found on pottery and rock carvings in Ancient Greece, dating from as early as 1800 BC.

With its simple V shape, the chevron pattern is a timeless design present in the art and fashion of cultures across the world, and today these stylish zigzag lines are found on every form of textile, including rugs, curtains, pillows, and wallpaper. Because of the ease with which chevrons are translated into new styles and colors, these patterns will continue to stay on trend, always appearing very modern.

1 African Batik 2 Chevron
3 Ikat 4 Kente 5 Serape
Rug 6 Kuba 7 Stripes
8 Tenango 9 Ndop cloth

For an expert mix, choose patterns in common colors. A sophisticated navy, black, and yellow color palette allows various patterns to live well together in this seating area.

THIS PAGE: Ikat prints make a statement. Oversize ikats in colors like hot pink will stand out. **OPPOSITE, ABOVE:** The chevron print on these X-benches adds a splash of pattern to a small space while tying into the color scheme of the bookshelf accessories. **OPPOSITE, BELOW:** Mix and match different cultural patterns with color in mind. Here, Kuba and ikat patterns in a similar palette complement each other nicely.

IKATS

When we sat down to create our initial textile collection, we developed a variety of prints to feature on our pillow line. One of the last prints we developed was a modern ikat pattern. In a bright yellow hue, the ikat print that we called "Haze" became the design for our most popular pillow, internally our most beloved design, and a real flagship pattern for the AphroChic brand. What's so interesting about ikat is that the design feels both cultural and new. Decorators everywhere are using the pattern in ways that make it one of today's most interesting motifs.

Like chevrons, ikat patterns are truly universal. With deep roots in the histories of Uzbekistan, Thailand, India, Japan, Indonesia, Nigeria, and Ivory Coast, this special technique of resist-dyeing (similar to tie-dyeing) fabrics may be one of the oldest forms of textile decoration. In many of these cultures, the use of ikat designs has been associated with status, prestige, and even magical powers.

Today, ikat is still one of our favorite patterns because of the way it can liven up a space, and it is one of the easiest ways to add ethnic identity to a room. And in today's trendiest colors, ikat prints blend tradition with a modern twist that's an excellent fit for current interiors.

KANGA

Almost a decade ago, we received our very own kanga fabric from a friend who had been traveling to Rwanda. The bold textile had a bright color palette of black, red, and yellow and a Swahili proverb inscribed on the side. It was the first African textile that we'd ever had in our home, and it started our love affair with African designs and the patterns and colors they can bring.

Kanga cloth has a two-hundred-year-old history that is truly diverse. Influenced by Swahili women, local Indian merchants, and American and British traders, kangas have been worn widely in East Africa as clothing or as head coverings for more than a century. Kanga cloth is often printed with phrases or proverbs in Swahili. Our own reads, *Huruma ninayo lakini sina bahati,* which translates into English as "Mercy I have, but luck I don't." A Swahili-speaking friend broke it down for us, and it roughly means "Even though I am blessed or fortunate, I still do not have luck." The translation is right up our alley: it's a great reminder to think about how blessed you are, even on days when you might not feel so lucky.

KANTHA QUILTS

Imagine a beautiful sari cloth from India. Now think about the remnants of vintage sari in varying shades of black, red, and orange, all stitched together to make a gorgeous quilt. That is the beauty of Indian kantha quilts, which have been woven for centuries by women from Bangladesh and West Bengal, India. The word *kantha* refers to the embroidery and "running stitch" design used on everything from mirrors to boxes and pillows in India.

Kantha quilts have taken on a particular significance over the past few years. These handmade pieces make absolutely beautiful bedding, throws, or wall hangings in a space where you want to bring in pattern, color, and texture.

KUBA

The Kuba are a group of people in the Democratic Republic of the Congo and the People's Republic of the Congo. They are known for weaving little squares or rectangles of material together to create garments. In the past, these garments signified a prestige reserved for kings, chiefs, and others of

OPPOSITE: For a modern touch, stick with accent pieces in traditional cultural patterns, such as this Kuba print cushion.

chic tip Fabric and cloth that you collect while traveling or visiting flea markets, or that may have been handed down in your family, can be used in a variety of ways beyond the realm of fashion. These pieces can be striking as tablecloths, bed coverings, curtains, and even wall art. For a fun DIY project, take a piece of cloth from your travels and hang it behind your bed as a makeshift headboard. Staple the fabric to a wooden frame or simply hang it on a rod. The bright shades and geometric patterns will add an artistic element to your bedroom décor.

high rank and were worn to designate their social status within the community. Today, while their fabrics are available to everyone, the fine, intricate embroidery of the Kuba definitely has a status all its own.

Many Kuba fabrics feature the abstract and geometric shapes that pay homage to traditional Kuba cloth. The designs are asymmetrical, irregular, and have a random feel to them, making them seem less formal and more like artistic or hand-drawn creations rather than a piece from a mass-produced line. This free-form pattern, which embraces geometric shapes and lines, lends a casual feel to a modern room.

STRIPES

These familiar lines may just be one of the world's earliest patterns. There's no question that stripes have some of the longest staying power of any motif in history. Sometimes skinny, sometimes bold, stripes have a universal appeal. Maybe it's because of the strong graphic image they present or the fact that they can be customized in hundreds of different styles and colors. Maybe it's because they are a classic design that always looks good. Whatever the appeal, stripes definitely have a place at home. And in different parts of the world, stripes in all of their many forms have taken on a number of cultural identities.

African kente cloth features nuanced stripe designs made by strip weaving. An important textile technique native to Ghana and Ivory Coast, this process involves interweaving to produce brightly colored textiles with distinct motifs and symbols. Within the fabric everything takes on meaning, especially the colors. Blue represents peace, harmony, and love; gold is associated with royalty and wealth; and maroon is the color of healing.

In Peru, striped rugs are also made by weaving colorful strips into a pattern. Weeks of meticulous hand looming can result in the most brightly colored striped rugs, with bits of purple, green, and yellow all in one fabulous floor covering.

In Mexico, serapes, blanket-like shawls worn by Mexican men in the eighteenth and nineteenth centuries, come in a variety of striped patterns. Using horizontal, vertical, or even diagonal and dotted lines, serape

A traditional piece of furniture is reincarnated when upholstered in today's most popular patterns. Black-and-white stripes transform an antique X-stool into a modern piece and turn a traditional Louis XIV chair into whimsical dining seating.

blankets boast some of the most intricate striped patterns that we have ever seen. So many lines are used, and in so many directions, that in some you will even spot a few chevrons.

TENANGO EMBROIDERIES

Tenangos are stunning works of indigenous art. A modern twist on traditional Mexican embroidery, tenangos are made by Mexico's Otomí Indians. Based upon centuries-old embellishments of costumes worn in the state of Hidalgo, the bright colors and brocade patterns were reinvented in the twentieth century with an embroidery process that includes common motifs found in nearby cave paintings. The word *tenango* means literally "stone neighborhood." Images of plants and animals are embroidered onto white fabric using brightly colored thread.

In the twenty-first century, these pieces have had a revival in the world of design. The works of the Otomí are now used as the most magnificent and eye-catching embroidered bedspreads. A favorite of interior designers, these coveted pieces can be highlighted as handmade art that can be hung on the wall or even brighten your bedding as a colorful bedspread.

DESIGNER PROFILE
malene b.
PUTS THE WORLD AT YOUR FEET

Designer Malene Barnett has a talent that few people possess. From any room in your home, Malene can whisk you away to the far corners of the earth—taking you from Bangkok to Bahia, Kingston to Kyoto, and back again. She can take you to market—let you feel the cool smoothness of a calabash beneath your fingers, or the rough texture of a beautiful African mask. She can even take you back in time, to walk the streets of Timbuktu, a center of learning that drew students from all over the world. That she can make all of this happen through her clever rug designs is a pretty cool trick.

With a base in Brooklyn, Malene's Caribbean ancestry, and a focus that encompasses the globe, the owner of Malene B Rugs does more than paint a pretty picture on your floor. Her designs are everything we look for in a rug: bold, colorful, and ultramodern, with absolutely stunning craftsmanship. Most of all, each rug is infused with a level of cultural significance that can create the vibe of a place or a culture instead of a direct reference. And as a big patterned piece, each rug's impact on a room's design and color palette is immediate and dramatic. (See Malene's home on page 206.)

The Mathematics of African Patterns

African textiles are works of art, entailing an amazing level of design sophistication. In many cases, they are also works of math, displaying an equally sharp grasp of the science of numbers. A large number of African patterns are fractal—that is, they are made up of shapes within shapes within shapes, sometimes with hundreds or thousands of iterations. These shapes and patterns are derived from African knowledge systems, such as the sand divination methods of the Bamana people of Mali.

The cultural, societal, and even political importance that these designs carry is staggering. Far beyond simple textile decoration, and far more than happenstance, these patterns have been used in everything from ritual garments to city planning. In fact, fractal organization schemes become visible in the layout of many African cities when viewed from above.

In the twelfth century, during the period of African control of southern Spain, African fractal patterns, specifically the Bamana divination method, and the math behind them moved through Africa into Europe,

where they were followed under the name *geomancy* (literally, "divination by earth"). By the seventeenth century, the basic concepts that these systems provided had influenced Catalan philosopher Raymond Lull, who in turn influenced German mathematician Gottfried Leibniz, the creator of binary code (which would later become the basis of all modern computer software).

Math and geometrics are inherently woven into African designs like Yoruba adire cloth, Fulani wedding blankets, and the various wares of the Mandiack weavers of Guinea-Bissau. With each textile, you are gaining not only something beautiful but patterned pieces with incredible thought and attention behind them, making them both works of art and a testimony to the knowledge of ancient people.

OPPOSITE: The fractals present in African textiles can produce beautiful pieces of patterned art. Kuba prints, kente cloth, Yoruba adire cloth, and other patterned pieces can be collected and framed to form a one-of-a-kind collection.

LEFT: Add cultural style to your living area by loading a sofa with a variety of suzani print cushions. OPPOSITE: It's easy to layer patterns in a room by adding a variety of textiles, from curtains to throws to pillows.

SUZANI

In the eighteenth and nineteenth centuries, suzanis were used as wall hangings, bedding, table linens, and even part of a bride's dowry. Having been a part of Uzbek homes for years, suzanis are now making their way into homes all over the world as textile art. The combination of bold patterns and warm colors fits perfectly with modern trends, making suzanis coveted decorative pieces. Today you can find suzani moon disk and floral motifs on decorative bedding and wall hangings, and on everyday textiles like pillows and upholstery.

The world is full of meaningful patterns. From every corner and every culture, designs have emerged and evolved, signifying everything from wealth to adulthood to inner peace. Bringing these patterns into your home is a way of paying homage to the cultures that you feel a special connection to. Even more, they are a means of curating a space that tells your story. But possibly the best thing about pattern when it comes to home décor is that there are so many ways use it. Textiles are one of the most common ways to introduce pattern in a space. They also happen to be our absolute favorite.

Mixing Patterns

Layering textiles is one of the easiest ways to mix and match patterns in your home. While the pieces themselves may be distinctive and represent different parts of the world, they can be bound together in your space through the use of a unifying "thread," which can be a similar shape, color, or even texture. In the end, the thread you choose (and there can be more than one) will matter less than the skill with which it is executed.

The best way to develop this skill is with trial and error. Test out a few combinations and see what looks best to you. To begin building an eclectic and cultural look, we suggest you start with three of your favorite patterned pieces; then consider the following tips for creating a great layered mix:

LEFT: A dining room chair features a bold pattern but in a neutral tone; it won't overwhelm the space. **OPPOSITE:** This neutral sofa featuring chevron upholstery adds visual texture and pattern without disrupting the bedroom's monochromatic color palette.

- Embrace patterned pieces in neutral tones. Choosing at least one patterned element in a neutral tone will allow you to fit it into your room without overwhelming the space.

- Identify patterned pieces that "speak" to one another. Do you like a curtain in a blue chevron pattern and a pillow in a blue ikat pattern? While the patterns may be different, the colors can communicate with and complement one another.

- Break up bright layers with furnishings in a single tone. A cream sofa or a black headboard is all you need to tone down patterns in a living room or a bedroom.

- Don't be afraid to mix it up. All the patterns you choose don't need to match. Instead, trying throwing in a piece or two that's completely different. It's fun to take risks and experiment with patterns, and you might find that you love an unexpected touch or two in the room you're decorating.

Combining different textile patterns in creative and interesting ways is one of the best things that you can do for your space. Every pattern is attached to a culture and has stories of its own beyond yours that can add a layer of character to your space and become a point of conversation when you're entertaining guests, or can just be something to muse over when relaxing quietly at home.

Using an assortment of textiles is one way to layer patterns for a sense of texture and depth in a room. The patterns present in this nature-inspired wallpaper pattern, striped alpaca throw, and the houndstooth pillows create a warm and cozy environment.

Pattern Your Floor with a Rug

A visit to one of our favorite places to shop, The Rug Company, shows just how cool rugs can be, especially when top fashion and interior designers like Diane von Fürstenberg and Martyn Lawrence-Bullard are involved. Patterned designs featuring bold florals, geometric shapes, and a mix of color and design can be seen throughout today's rug collections. Recently, we've also seen a revival of traditional rugs sporting sophisticated patterns and cultural appeal. From the dhurries of India, to Persian kilims, and Moroccan handiras, these types of rugs offer the most distinctive, eye-catching designs, adding warmth to an interior and layers of personal style. There are tons of beautiful rug options out there to explore, but when looking for something with cultural style, check out these patterned floor coverings that evoke ancient and far-off places:

DHURRIES

These hand-loomed floor coverings traditionally hail from India. Flat-woven from natural materials like cotton, wool, jute, or silk, dhurries are more than just rugs for the home. They have been used in everything from meditation to special décor for social gatherings. You can spot them at some of your favorite stores, such as West Elm.

KILIMS

Over the past few years, kilims have popped up in both modern and traditional homes. Originating from a rich tradition of textile design that dates back thousands of years (some believe as far back as 4000 BC), kilims are truly global pieces of art. Present in the design cultures of North Africa, Turkey, Iran, Pakistan, Central Asia, and China, these flat-woven textiles similar to dhurries contain a variety of patterns and colors in just one piece, making them the perfect way to add cultural pattern to spaces where you want a big impact. Check out the home section of eclectic stores like Anthropologie for a selection of unique and modern kilims.

ABOVE, LEFT TO RIGHT: Use dhurries and kilims to introduce fractal and geometric patterns to your interior. An overdyed rug in a vibrant color like crimson can be a stunning patterned piece. Moroccan Beni Ourain rugs feature intricate patterns on a neutral backdrop—perfect for quiet spaces, like bedrooms.

MOROCCAN RUGS

Moroccan Beni Ourain and Boucherouite rugs are coveted in today's interiors for their beautiful patterns and colors. Our favorites are Moroccan wedding capes, known as handiras, that were worn by brides during Berber wedding ceremonies in Morocco. Crafted by the women of the bride's family, each sequin and patterned strip of fabric is hand-sewn to the cape. The objects attached to the handira are more than just decoration: they're blessings, prayers, and wishes of fertility and good luck for the bride and groom. Today, these traditional wedding garments are taking on new roles as décor. You can find them in a variety of shades. Beyond the typical cream ones, we have spotted them in black, blue, and even pink and bright yellow. Finding our own handira was an experience we will always treasure. Jeanine was exploring a favorite blog, *My Marrakesh*, when she spotted one, and had it shipped directly from Morocco to our home. It has been a favorite piece of ours, used at times as a bed throw and then as a carpet in our home office, and it adds just the right amount of sparkle, texture, and pattern to any room we place it in.

chic tip Rugs are an investment, so when introducing one with bold pattern and color—like a Moroccan wedding cape or an antique kilim—let it be the star of the room. To help it fit into the design of your space, try to lift a shade you like from the rug and match it with a few other elements in your room, like a pillow or a throw.

OVERDYED TURKISH RUGS

The concept is innovative; the results are unbelievably beautiful. Overdyed Turkish rugs are one-of-a-kind pieces that put a twist on tradition and embrace eco-friendly design. Turkish designers remove the original color from vintage rugs and then overdye them to create vibrant carpets. The final result is a classic piece veiled by jewel-tone hues like neon pink, electric green, opulent red, and saturated yellow.

Overdyed rugs can transform your interior by adding the pop of color it needs while still ushering in the beauty of traditional Turkish rug design. Modern and classic, these rugs have it all. Our favorite place to shop for these color-reformed pieces is at ABC Carpet & Home, which has a beautiful collection.

RIGHT: Using a bold pattern can enliven an entire space. Stylist Emily Henderson used our chevron print wallpaper, called "The Vibe," to add an energetic feel to this living room. **OPPOSITE:** Go beyond the accent wall and design a statement room with a bold and colorful wallpaper pattern that envelopes the entire space. This red, pink, and gold floral design sets the tone for a romantic entryway.

Create a Statement with Wallpaper

Though textiles are by far the most versatile way to bring pattern into your space, they are just as far from being your only option. There are much bigger statements of pattern to be made in the right places. Wallpaper is an often-underrated component of the patterned mix. Not so long ago, wallpaper had fallen out of favor with most designers for several reasons. It was difficult to put up, the patterns were boring, and wallpapered interiors just looked outdated. But over the last few years, wallpaper has been making a major comeback. With an infusion of young designers, it has moved beyond the fancy showrooms of the past and is now easily accessible through online boutiques and curators of the latest in design. Daring, whimsical, and thought-provoking patterns can be found in a range of trendy colors and in unique water-based and metallic inks.

Today's wallpaper offerings are more customizable than ever before, making it easy for you to find the perfect patterned backdrop that you can customize in your favorite hue. Or if you're feeling really bold, you can take a photo or a design of your very own and have it turned into wallpaper through custom manufacturers like DesignYourWall .com. This website allows you to design your own wall mural using a favorite family photo or a photo from a trip that you'll always want to remember.

Finding the right wallpaper can help you create a room with the sense of culture and personality you're going for. While paint can help set the tone at home, patterned wallpaper can add new dimensions to the textiles and other patterned elements in your home. And like textiles, patterned wallpaper has the profound ability to tell a cultural story. The potential wow factor of combining bold colors with cultural patterns has not been lost on wallpaper manufacturers. Today many companies offer unique wallpapers that feature distinctive and modern patterns based on traditional Kuba prints, Moroccan tiles, and even funky chevrons.

chic tip A busy wallpaper pattern may not be the best fit for your entire room but can make an impact in small doses. Choose a bold and energizing pattern for an accent wall or entryway. You can even frame a piece of wallpaper and turn it into a work of art. When you are wallpapering the entire room, a pattern in a neutral shade may be just right. A geometric print in all black can have a luxurious look, and the single hue can keep the room looking cohesive.

CHOOSE WALLPAPER THAT SETS THE TONE

Wallpaper transforms rooms. Just a few rolls can make a space look larger, brighter, and filled with personality that it didn't have before. Choosing the right kind of paper is key. Start with the elements in the room: Is there a pattern or color that can serve as inspiration for the kind of paper you are looking for?

With that inspirational piece in mind, source papers that fit, either by pattern or by color, in your interior. Thinking about the emotions, places, or cultures you want to convey is the best guide to making sure you pick the right paper for your walls.

RIGHT: Drama has been added to this bathroom with a gold-and-purple wallpaper design that covers the room—even the ceiling. **OPPOSITE:** Using wallpaper in a small way can create big impact. Just one panel of Fornasetti wallpaper in this living room adds a cool artistic detail.

ACCENT WALLS VERSUS WALLPAPERED ROOMS

The biggest decision you will have to make with wallpaper is whether or not to decorate the entire room. Choosing to bring attention to a single wall can be both beautiful and budget-friendly. Accent walls can highlight a specific part of a room, delineate an area in an open-plan space, or bring attention to a standout piece of furniture.

Wallpaper doesn't have to end with just an accent. Instead of creating a single point of interest within your room, wallpaper can serve as the backdrop for the entire space. Enveloping a room in pattern can be incredibly dramatic. Oversized florals, Indian block prints, and even textured patterns can all be used to create a breathtaking space defined by the motif on each wall.

Whether you have roots in Mexico or Peru, Africa or Europe, patterned textiles, wallpaper, and accessories are an important component in creating a global mix at home that will help you tell a more individual story—one about a celebration of diversity, embracing cultural motifs, and identifying unique ways to make them your own.

3
ORIGINAL
ART

Lady Bird Johnson famously remarked that art is a window into the soul, one that permits us to observe the world beyond

ourselves while giving us the chance to better understand one another through the vision of the artist. It's an assessment we've taken to heart while considering the place of art in our cultures, our lives, and our homes. Living with art is one of the biggest steps you can take toward creating a home with soulful style. Without art to complete the décor, no home ever feels quite finished. Pieces created by you, for you, or that you have discovered and connected with are a must-have. The art you display in your home is a direct expression of who you are. Each piece speaks to some aspect of your personal experience and perspective while simultaneously relating those ideas to everyone who enters.

As with so much else at AphroChic, our love of art is inspired by our own cultural heritage. In Jeanine's childhood home, no room was ever decorated without hanging a favorite art print as a finishing touch. As a teenager, she even commissioned a few pieces from the budding artists in her high school classes to keep for herself.

When Bryan was growing up, his mother's love of art was a constant theme throughout the house. To this day, she has a number of paintings culled from many different sources hanging on her walls. Our favorite is a print by Jamaican artist Bernard Stanley Hoyes, *One Vision*, which depicts Dr. Martin Luther King Jr. and Malcolm X looking out through a shared eye. The colorful and imaginative work is an example of an idea that has always been a part of our experience with art: that living with art is important not only for decorating but for expressing a cultural point of view as well.

With the *AphroChic* blog came an opportunity to share and explore our love of art with a large online audience. The "Original Art" series was created to help lead readers to discover works by a diverse com-

PREVIOUS AND OPPOSITE: Purchase original paintings and works that you identify with. Don't buy paintings for their investment potential; instead, spring for beautiful pieces that can fit seamlessly into your interior.

munity of up-and-coming artists. The ability of art not only to reference a culture but to openly communicate a point of view is what we find so exciting. When art holds a message that expresses a personal perspective or the shared experiences of a cultural group—that is when it is most exhilarating. Building your art collection can be as simple as finding a few key pieces, or a lifelong endeavor of acquiring and curating pieces that you love in a variety of mediums. Painting, photography, mixed media, and illustration are a few of our favorite ways to bring art with soul into a home.

Bring In Paintings

Few art forms are as expressive and evocative as what results when a brush touches the canvas. Perhaps that's why so few arts compare in the sheer range of philosophies,

techniques, and subject matter: there are nearly as many schools of painting as there are artists at the task. And as a result, there is no larger field to explore when searching for works that speak to you.

In addition to the air of sophistication that paintings can bring to your interior, they can also be used to infuse a monochromatic space with color. Even in rooms with a strong color story, paintings can often contribute by picking up trends in your color palette in a way that is sometimes less evident than with sculptures or photographs. Whether composed in black and white, muted earth tones, or a mix of neon colors, these pieces are not only on display but are numbered among the accessories of your home, adding color, texture, and depth to the interior.

If you're searching for new art, exploring your hometown can often take you into galleries where you'll find the latest in portraits, abstracts, and modern paintings. It's also important to go off the beaten path. Check out the student exhibitions

ABOVE: Use paintings to brighten up your home. Here, artist Nicole Cohen showcases her own abstract paintings. The mix of colors on this canvas creates a unique color story in an otherwise neutral room. **LEFT:** This painting of an African woman is a beautiful display of cultural style, with vivid colors and an abstract pattern. **OPPOSITE:** *The Screaming Lady* by Yahgie captures the glamorous, feminine style in this modern interior.

RIGHT: Art lover Joy Simmons collects pieces from up-and-coming artists. This piece by Stephen Namara is one of many works by artists she discovered at student exhibits and local galleries. **OPPOSITE:** Allow the art in your home to speak to a room's décor, or vice versa. The forest in this painting mimics the direction of the chevron print in the curtains.

at your local art schools. Some of these pieces are affordable and may represent the work of a major artist in the making. More than one of the works that caught our eye as we toured the homes in this book were acquired through chance encounters with big names before they were stars.

And while you're out searching for the world's next Warhol or Basquiat, remember that it's not only the newest works that may pique your interest or touch your heart. Older works that are new to you deserve your attention as well. Flea markets and vintage shops are great places to find paintings with a history. There, any number of forgotten treasures can be found after long years trapped in basements and attics. These pieces are often very affordable (especially when you come across a gem that the seller doesn't know about!), and bringing these old works home can add new life to your space.

Finally, whether you've mastered the fine art of painting or only dabbled a little, don't be afraid to bring out some of your own pieces to show off at home. Showcasing your own work is a great way to ensure that your collection will always speak to you. There is nothing more personal than something you have created yourself.

COLLECTOR'S PROFILE

joy simmons: A CURATED LIFE

Socrates famously mused that, for a human being, "the unexamined life is not worth living." The same could likely be said for a life without passion. Los Angeles–based art collector Joy Simmons is in danger of neither. Two things are apparent upon stepping into her gorgeous home: first, that she has done a lot of thinking about who she is and, second, that her true passion is African American art.

As a student at Stanford University, Joy received an extracurricular education that many art history majors would have envied. Every summer Joy would travel to New York to visit relatives. Her uncle, Ron Carter, is a famed jazz bassist known for recording with such artists as Lena Horne, George Benson, and B.B. King, among others. Her aunt, Janet Carter, was a founding board member and trustee of the Studio Museum in Harlem. She was a lifelong advocate for African and African American art, and she shared that love with her niece.

It was Janet who first got Joy interested in art beyond the Jimi Hendrix posters that hung in her dorm room. "She started to talk to me about collecting," Joy recalls, "and had me thinking about my own collection in a thoughtful way."

It didn't take long for Joy to acquire her first piece. As she transitioned into medical school at UCLA, she picked up an Elizabeth Catlett work entitled *Which Way*. Though it has since been joined by hundreds of other pieces of African American art, this inaugural acquisition still hangs in Joy's bedroom—a reminder of the beginning of a lifelong journey.

Joy's collection is as much an exploration of identity as it is a labor of love. "What I purchase adds to the language of contemporary African American art," she says—and the conversation is ongoing. On the first floor alone, a Warhol depicting Queen Ntombi of Swaziland hangs in the kitchen, while a Kehinde Wiley sketch unobtrusively adorns a wall in the corridor. Meanwhile works from Mickalene Thomas and Kara Walker converse in a living room specifically conceived with art in mind right down to the gallery-quality lighting that illuminates each piece.

A successful radiologist, Joy attended courses in architecture and construction at UCLA and Los Angeles Community College before designing her perfect home. Standing in the picturesque Ladera Heights district, a historically affluent African American community, the Simmons house is equal parts residence and museum—the perfect showcase for her ever-growing collection.

While many of her pieces have famous names attached to them, Joy is a committed talent scout. Many of the works she owns are by young artists under the age of thirty. She believes in looking for new artists locally and is more than willing to take a chance on potential masterpieces.

One such expansive work—a mural that covers most of her back deck and the doorway that leads to it—Joy commissioned from a local Los Angeles artist. At the same time, she also commissioned a collaboration between Varnette Honeywood—an artist popularly known for the appearance of her pieces on *The Cosby Show*—and a local stained glass designer, whose combined work created the stunning vignette that decorates her front door.

Joy's love of art has always focused on bringing attention to the work of African American artists, with a particular focus on finding and nurturing the future stars of artistic expression. "Art is a way of telling a story about our culture," she remarks simply. "Artists are telling the story of our time."

Here is Joy's list of her favorite places to find African American art:

- **California African American Museum (Los Angeles)**
- **Studio Museum in Harlem**
- **African American Museum of Philadelphia**
- **Detroit African American Museum**
- **Oakland Museum of California**
- **San Francisco Museum of Modern Art (SFMOMA)**
- **Yerba Buena Center for the Arts (San Francisco)**
- **Diaspora Vibe Gallery (Miami)**
- **Art Basel Miami Beach**
- **Museum of African Art (Los Angeles)**

LEFT: Joy Simmons commissioned Oakland muralist Keith Williams to create an original work for her patio. **CENTER:** Thin sheets of stainless steel have been cut to form a sculptural chandelier in the dining room. **RIGHT:** Joy welcomes guests with art even as they walk through the door. She worked with African American artist Varnette Honeywood to design special glass doors for her entryway.

Curate a Photography Collection

A picture may tell a thousand words, but a good photograph can speak volumes. Capturing fleeting moments in pristine condition, photography has the potential to add plenty of soul to your space. Moreover, photos are often easier to collect than paintings, making them a great choice if you're looking to start an extensive collection.

Photos are storytelling pieces. And with just a few of the right pictures, you can fill your interior with any story that intrigues you—even your own.

You can purchase professional images for your home at a number of sites online (check out our Resources). And don't forget about your favorite furniture stores. Many have an art section where you can leaf through bins of available prints. Finally, frame shops are a great source for professional work. Many will have a selection of images you can choose from and then have framed and matted right there.

ABOVE: A collection of black-and-white photos is a perfect storytelling piece for your evolving art collection. Curate your own Gordon Parks–style works with black-and-white images of friends, family, and your favorite icons. **OPPOSITE:** For large-scale photographic prints, work with a professional framer to create a unique frame.

You can choose anything, from pictures of your favorite celebrities to classic images. Once the arrangement is complete, your family images will be elevated to a spectacular black-and-white collection of pieces that inspire you and that will always bring back special memories.

Another benefit to photography is its growing accessibility. Today the right technology to capture that perfect image is never far away. With increasingly powerful digital cameras and a huge number of apps for editing, it's getting easier and easier to take a fantastic photo with something as small as an iPhone. And the growing number of image-sharing social media platforms means that anyone can create a photography collection with charming snapshots taken while traveling for vacation or just walking down the street. Get outside and snap away on your camera phone. When you get home, print out your shots and place them in your favorite picture frames. You will have the makings of a beautiful visual collection that's completely and totally you.

A collection of photographic prints can be a way to express a personal point of view in your home. Art collector Joy Simmons fills her home with African American art that carries socio-political messages. Many offer important insights into the African American experience. Look for intriguing art that expresses your own experience.

A Legacy of African American Art

Art has been a part of the African American experience from the very beginnings of the culture—as crafts and methods were imported from Africa and European methods were adapted to the myriad experiences of African Americans, new expressions began to emerge. From the seventeenth through the nineteenth centuries, enslaved Africans, many of whom were skilled artisans, created functional pieces like drums, quilts, and ceramic vessels in addition to working with both wood and metal.

Following the Civil War, the works of African American painters began to gain notice. Henry Ossawa Tanner's works were exhibited in cities around the world, including Philadelphia, where the artist first trained. Later, the arrival of the Roaring Twenties in American popular culture coincided with an unprecedented upsurge of creativity in the African American community in the midst of the Great Migration out of the rural South.

This rising tide of inspiration culminated in the movement now remembered as the Harlem Renaissance. During that notable time, which had parallels in France and elsewhere, African American culture entered (for the first time without caricature) into mainstream American culture through every available medium, not the least of which was visual art. Led by luminaries such as Aaron Douglas, Palmer Hayden, Loïs Mailou Jones, and Romare Bearden, the art of the Harlem Renaissance was a critical reimagining of popular images of African American life with themes and motifs that continue to speak to us nearly a century later.

Jones showcased the lives of middle-class African Americans through pieces like *Jennie,* a portrait of a young woman preparing a family meal. Bearden used collage, watercolors, oils, photomontage, and prints to reflect on his own past as well as on historic events. His piece *The Lamp* commemorated the thirtieth anniversary of the US Supreme Court's decision to end segregation in public schools.

Through the 1960s and 1970s, African American art continued to capture the political changes of the time, documenting the shared experiences of African Americans during the Civil Rights and Black Power movements. The radical, confrontational, and captivating art of the period is epitomized in works such as those of Emory Douglas from California, whose art adorned nearly every publication of the Black Panther Party.

As the minister of culture for the Black Panthers, Douglas was an important member of one of the most iconic organizations of the Black Power movement. The social impact of his illustrations and collages has been compared to that of Norman Rockwell for their role in documenting the struggles of African American life during the 1960s and '70s.

On the East Coast, the Harlem-based Weusi group formed around a philosophy of cultural consciousness, community outreach, and the promotion of a positive Black aesthetic through the visual arts. The Weusi group was responsible for opening the Weusi Nyumba Ya Sanaa Gallery and Academy of African Arts and Studies in Harlem during the same period in the late 1960s that the National Center of Afro-American Artists in Boston, the Anacostia Neighborhood Museum in Washington, DC, and the Studio Museum in Harlem were all founded.

The importance of art to African American culture continues today as new artists find innovative ways of speaking to the changing experiences of their communities. Techniques like the cut-paper-silhouette murals of Kara Walker and the stunningly iconic portraits of African American males by Kehinde Wiley breathe new life into the stories that African Americans continue to tell. Their work continues a dialogue for exploring the full potential and meaning of experiences past and present as we work toward the future.

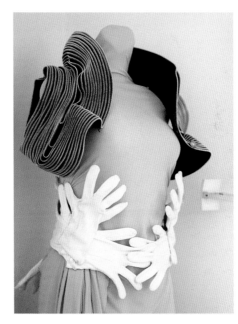

Joy Simmons arranged this piece to show off an innovative glove belt by designer Jan Mandel. Accompanied by a stylish vest acquired in Soho, the combination turns a simple mannequin into fashion-forward art.

Explore Mixed Media Art

The fusion of two or more artistic mediums can create a number of interesting possibilities for your home. In our opinion, these are some of the coolest pieces you can hang on your walls. With layers, texture, and often hidden meanings, mixed-media collages offer an eclectic mix that can exist in just one piece.

Many artists have used mixed media to express social and even political ideas. African American artists have often used a combination of techniques to highlight the internal struggles and changing nature of African American identity, as well as to document political progress. Jeff Donaldson, a cofounder of the renowned Chicago-based group AFRICOBRA (African Commune of Bad Relevant Artists), uses his work as a way of declaring his heritage, creating pieces that speak to a range of topics, including African spiritualism and soul music. Others, like Philadelphia-born artist Len Davis, use found objects and printouts to create images of African American men that are surrounded by hidden messages about race and identity. And Dutch designer Menno Schmitz has brought his talents to New York, creating mixed-media collages comprised of silk

screens, shawls, and banners, depicting images of African women and currency. For depth, layers, and even a bit of social commentary, these pieces are sure to add something unique to your interior.

Express Your Personal Style with Illustrations

Illustrations are wonderful and very affordable pieces that can either add to your existing art collection or form the basis of a gallery of their own. They are a great way to reimagine classic motifs for home décor. In our Brooklyn Renaissance collection, we teamed up with New York artist Samantha Hahn, to create watercolor illustrations of a series of fashionably modern city girls rocking afros, riding Vespas, and living in brownstones—images which expressed our point of view through a celebration of urban women. What's so appealing about illustrations for decorating at home is the

ABOVE: Mixed-media pieces are a great way to introduce the unexpected to your art collection. Visit sites such as Etsy, independent art shows, and local galleries to find works like this hand-painted telephone. **LEFT:** Look for affordable prints and mixed media on canvas, such as this print featuring a photo of Naomi Campbell, painted graffiti, and an illustration of the Brooklyn Bridge. **OPPOSITE:** Here, vinyl records have been laser-cut into butterflies to form an innovative mixed-media piece installed so that it appears to fly off the wall.

simple-yet-sophisticated aesthetic they lend to a space. Creating captivating images that still leave plenty of room for guests to read between the lines, fashion illustrations provide an instant update to any subject. Whether you're looking for a portrait, a landscape, or a toile, illustration is a great technique for making a traditional approach feel fresh and new.

Keep a lookout for affordable prints that are available online. A few simple picture frames is all it takes for these illustrations to become a fantastic wall display. You can also find unique illustrations on textiles like pillows—and even on your favorite tableware. Jeanine loves plates featuring this runway-born style. Most important, have fun finding cool pieces that uniquely express you.

ABOVE: Every room in the home can be used to showcase a diverse art collection. A mix of illustrations, paintings, textile art, and photographs creates a vivid installation of unique works in this bedroom. **OPPOSITE:** In this Manhattan home, a child's illustration is elevated to a work of art. Placed in a simple black-and-white frame, it's part of the home's unique art collection.

1 DESIGNERS ARE MEANT TO BE **LOVED** NOT TO BE UNDERSTOOD

THE PURPOSE OF DESIGN IS TO MAKE THE ORDINARY EXTRAORDINARY **2** **6**

3 THE BEST DESIGNERS ARE THE ONES WHO FIND THE **GOOD CLIENTS**

DESIGN MUST SEDUCE, SHAPE & MORE IMPORTANTLY, EVOKE AN **EMOTIONAL** **4** **RESPONSE**

GOOD DESIGN CAN BE PLANNED BUT **GREAT DESIGN** **5** **JUST HAPPENS**

DESIGN THE RIGHT THINGS DESIGN THE THINGS RIGHT

IMAGINATION 7 IS MORE IMPORTANT THAN KNOWLEDGE

THE 7 RULES TO UNDERSTAND DESIGN & DESIGNERS

Sourcing Art Online

Thanks to the Internet, a global search for art never has to leave your living room. We still recommend visiting galleries and art shows for a unique experience, but if you're not finding what you're looking for, the web offers a number of options, whether you're searching for paintings and photos or something more exotic.

Curated art sites like Artaissance and Art.com are fantastic resources for identifying fine paintings, decorative pieces, and vintage art and photography. These sites focus on categorization, making it easy to search by genres or by a specific color to find a piece that is perfect for the room you are decorating.

Look at sites like Howkapow, Gallery Hanahou, and Society6, for limited-edition works. Searching for one-of-a-kind or limited-edition pieces can take more time, but it makes the work that much more special. Also, be sure to see if the site offers customization options—a must for interior design. If you're going for the art gallery look, you can print your work on canvas, or go very modern and mount it on acrylic. The number of options available on online art sites will make designing your collection an exercise in creative expression.

One of our favorite places for sourcing the work of independent artists, Etsy brings to you a massive virtual marketplace of professionals, artisans, hobbyists, and independent artists, where you can discover handmade and vintage work from around the world. Great finds can often be spotted for as little as $20 or $30 a print. The site includes the work of thousands of contributors working in a variety of disciplines. We suggest using specific keywords to streamline your searches. Then it only takes a few quick clicks to start a unique collection you can build over time.

DISCOVER ARTISTS IN THE BLOGOSPHERE

Featuring the work of up-and-coming artists is something that we do regularly on our blog, and we suggest looking at art and design blogs as resources to find buzz-worthy pieces and the newest offerings from artists around the globe. Following a local art and design blog is also a great way to be in the loop about upcoming events in your community and even national events like Art Basel Miami Beach, the National Black Arts Festival, and various gallery openings.

OPPOSITE: Typographic art is a great way to bring new fonts and messages into your art collection. You can find a variety of pieces with inspirational messages, quotes, and manifestos by searching online art sites.

LEFT: This homeowner has highlighted personal photographs by creating a salon wall in the entryway. Group a variety of pieces together in different sizes for a collected look. **OPPOSITE:** Place small sculptures, photography, and tchotchkes on bookshelves. This shelving unit is the perfect backdrop for the homeowner's rotating collection of miniature art.

Ideas for Showcasing Your Collection

Whether art collecting has been a lifelong hobby or you're just getting started, there are a number of different ways to showcase your art collection, from multipiece salon walls to minimal shelving units that hold only a couple of works apiece. Choosing the right format can depend on a few different factors, such as whether you intend to keep the design static or to rotate your pieces in and out of the room from time to time. But no matter what size or type of collection you have, you can design a unique way to showcase and highlight work that is important to you.

For a rotating collection of paintings and prints, we love the idea of placing a few pieces on a slim shelving unit. Floating wall shelves with a simple ledge can highlight

Mix art among your books. Stack pieces in front of books and make room on the shelves for an artsy collection.

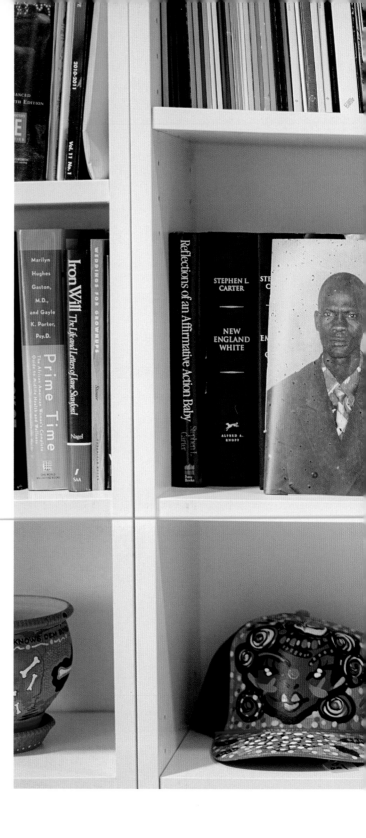

Showcase a few distinct pieces of art in a single vignette. Here, a Jimmy Cliff poster becomes a framed art print and is coupled with an original photograph and collection of gold Seletti containers. Look for unique pieces you can highlight in shadow boxes. These white boxing gloves featuring the words EVERFORWARD and NEVERBACK are a unique piece of mixed-media art. Place art in unconventional places: a piano can be the perfect location for works in an expansive collection.

your favorite works while giving you the flexibility to change the assortment whenever you like. Mix in some small accessories like handmade pottery, carvings, or sculptures to add to the artistic feel.

When wall space is limited, be innovative and use another backdrop for your collection. With nails and a few hooks (or even a sturdy adhesive hook), you can install art on a bookshelf. Changing out pieces is quick and easy, and attaching your art to the bookshelf leaves no damage on walls, making it the perfect way to hang art in your apartment and keep your security deposit. Art can even be placed on the floor for a less formal-looking collection. Simply layer your pieces and lean them against the wall. Not only is it unexpected, it's also another easy way to rotate and rearrange pieces at will.

While we're big fans of a collection of frames for an art gallery, oversized pieces are also an excellent way to create an exceptional look. Two or three big pieces hung together will make a quite a statement. With big prints, a little goes a long way, so make sure that your pieces complement each other in terms of color, technique, or design to maintain a cohesive look. Oversized pieces affect everything else in the room, so choose ones that fit into your overall color palette without creating an overload of pattern.

Protecting Your Art

When purchasing photography, prints, and paintings that need to be framed, be sure to buy frames that protect your work from fading and decay:

- Acid-free mat boards can help reduce yellowing and fading. Professional framers and art stores sell mats in a variety of sizes, so you can find the best mat board to fit your work.

- When hanging your art, be sure not to expose pieces to direct sunlight. Images can be damaged by heat, UV rays, and high humidity.

- Look for picture frames that can protect your work from UV light. Specialized conservation glass can protect work that is hung in areas with a lot of light.

Creating a Salon Wall

A salon wall is a wonderful way to give your collection of various prints and paintings the proper art gallery treatment. To create a wall display of your favorite pieces, there are just a few steps you need to follow:

STEP 1: Choose your favorite art pieces. A salon wall has only so much space, so be sure to grab the ones that you can't wait to hang up. They don't all have to be the same size or use the same colors. A hodgepodge effect is welcome, so you can get creative and bring together a mix of prints, photos, and even collected pieces like album covers that can serve as beautiful statement pieces.

STEP 2: With some kraft paper (or newspaper), a pencil, scissors, a hammer, nails, and easily removable tape,

you can begin creating the layout for your wall. Place the art on the kraft paper or newspaper on the floor and decide on the best visual layout. Then outline the pieces.

STEP 3: Label the shapes of your artwork, and then hang the paper on the wall using painter's tape or even Japanese washi tape, which can be easily be removed without stripping the wall paint.

STEP 4: Now it's time to hang the actual art. Mark on the kraft paper where the nail will go, and hammer in the nail. Once the nail is securely in place, take down the paper, and hang your piece.

STEP 5: Continue until all the pieces are in place, and your salon wall is complete.

4

GLOBAL
OBJECTS

In this age of rapid and pervasive globalization, the modern interior celebrates international style and ethnic diversity.

We love looking at styles from around the world for inspiration—mixing and matching them and bringing international furnishings and accessories into every part of the home. Global accessories bring a sense of adventure to modern design by weaving a narrative of journeys both real and imagined.

Our love for design from all over the world is as much based on our own cultural history as on our admiration for other histories. African American culture is a global culture. Like every civilization of the African Diaspora, it is both a consequence of and a monument to the intersection of cultures across oceans and national boundaries. As we work to further cultivate our AphroChic brand, the history of African American culture—its creation, development, and successes around the globe—continues to inspire and remind us to include the world in our design stories.

As modern design becomes ever more a mix of global influences, the key to creating soulful spaces is in choosing cultural pieces that are stylish but also have meaning. While the freedom to choose between diverse offerings from around the world was once a luxury reserved for royalty, today many more of us can pick and choose from the multitude of artisans and styles available today to find the perfect pieces to fill in our own stories.

Global Pieces for Modern Spaces

In a world where items are imported and exported daily, nearly every home accessory or piece of furniture can be considered global to some extent. Yet certain pieces stand outside the mainstream furniture mix, pieces that have a true sense of identity expressed through remarkable craftsmanship and often through traditions that have been passed down for hundreds of years. These pieces, whether antiques, reproductions, or modern

THIS PAGE: Global objects can add design and interest to a modern space. Here, Moroccan lanterns are hung as elegant pendant lighting in this modern kitchen. With sculptural shapes and intricate designs, these lanterns bring chic global style into this home. PREVIOUS PAGE: In this dining nook, a citron, brown, and pink color palette unifies cultural objects and modern furnishings.

RIGHT: Bring back small pieces from your travels to start a global collection. Small carvings and sculptures from flea markets and souks can be displayed at home on bookshelves, coffee tables, and mantels. **OPPOSITE:** Place global pieces like wood carvings on an open and airy shelving unit to showcase your collection. This white shelving in a space designed by Emily Henderson is a perfect contrast to the heavy wood carvings that have been placed in cubbies on the shelves.

interpretations, have a timeless design that is also tied to a national identity. African stools, Indian chairs, and Chinese cabinets are all examples of traditional items that when worked into today's modern spaces become statement pieces, whether we're speaking to our own heritages or providing a basis for interaction with cultures from half a world away.

When working with global furnishings, look for pieces that:

- HAVE A SCULPTURAL DESIGN. They will be a nice enhancement to modern interiors, which tend to have plenty of straight, hard lines. Sculptural furnishings will soften the lines and add an artistic element to the room.

- ARE MADE FROM NATURAL ELEMENTS. Look for hand-carved or naturally woven pieces, wood furnishings, and sculptures. The natural element will add warmth and texture into a modern space.

- GO BEYOND THEMES. While ideas of "Safari Chic" or "Passage to India" may seem trendier than traditional furnishings, look for pieces that are not thematic but rather speak to your own individual style. Before adding "exotic" pieces to your interior, try to learn something about the culture they represent, the tradition they come from, and the meaning they carry. This information can only strengthen your interaction with these pieces and enhance your experience of the space they occupy.

DESIGNER PROFILE

boa: A SILK ROAD RUNS THROUGH BROOKLYN

Nestled away in a quiet corner of our favorite New York borough, furniture designer BOA blends influences from all over the world to create designer pieces that meet a new standard of modernity. BOA tells us, "Most people confuse modern with popular. They are not the same thing." In BOA's view, popular is trendy, and trends change every few years, sometimes from season to season. That which is truly modern, however, is timeless. Good modern design transcends trends in order to remain relevant decades or even centuries after its first appearance.

BOA's work is sleek, clean, and low. Her collections include tables, seating, mirrors, beds, shelves, and cabinets. Over the years, her early predilection for straight lines has given way to a preference for smooth curves that emphasize the femininity of her ideas. Feeling that she is at her best as an artist when incorporating nature into her pieces, BOA strives to maintain the organic elements of the materials in her work, emphasizing the visual texture of wood grains even when presenting pieces in their cleanest and most streamlined forms. This deep respect for nature pervades her design aesthetic, even to the choice of materials she uses. Recycled and repurposed materials such as sorghum stock, recycled aluminum, and fiber made from plastic bottles are common elements of her pieces.

BOA herself is a study in transnational movement and culture. A native of Saint John in the US Virgin Islands, the model-turned-furniture-designer has lived and traveled all over the world, studying design in Chicago and traveling in Europe before settling, if only intermittently, in New York. As a devout student of Buddhist and Hindu philosophies, BOA calls Southeast Asia her spiritual home. This mix of influences is evident in many of her pieces, which either display Buddhist motifs or simply evoke a peaceful sensibility.

The ultimate goal of BOA's designs is to blur the line that Western culture places between art and everyday life. She believes that the tables we sit at and the chairs we sit on should be as beautiful as any painting and as meaningful as the various patterns, textiles, and potteries developed by traditional cultures around the world. The functionality that BOA programs into her pieces is an active engagement with the way that people live.

In her search for the eternal "now" in her work, BOA creates pieces that meet her own high expectations for what's modern—timeless and functional, a blend of high art and everyday life at peace with the world around it. With wares evoking the traditions of Africa, Asia, and Europe, BOA's Brooklyn workshop has become the newest stop along the Silk Road. (See BOA's home on page 190.)

Global Furnishings That We Love

Furniture is one of the biggest decisions you will make in your space. Just down from the floors and walls in terms of scale, furniture pieces can hold the most color and carry the most pattern, making them among the best places to start when going for a global look and feel. Combined, pieces from the same region can whisk you away to some far corner of the world, while mixing pieces from various locales can infuse your space with an air of quiet sophistication.

Gather an eclectic mix of global objects together with ease by using similar shapes or colors. A Chinese gourd lamp and bamboo cane bench sit among European chairs and traditional American furnishings in this seating area where everything has a common color palette.

There are no rules on where to begin when looking to globalize your furniture collection. We tend to begin with the pieces we spend the most time with—the pieces that are our first stop after a long day and our last stop on a lazy weekend.

Global pieces have been layered into this space to create an African-inspired bedroom. The shape of the window coverings resembles Moroccan-style archways. A pair of West African Senufo stools becomes extra seating at the foot of the bed, and block-print cushions add to the lively global mix.

RIGHT: Be on the lookout for non-traditional poufs. This floral pouf has the same shape and size as the traditional Moroccan seating but is adorned with wool flowers for a unique look and texture.
OPPOSITE: A hand-knitted pouf adds whimsy and texture to this contemporary living room. Find poufs like this one on Etsy.

SEATING

Where and how we sit, relax, and recline has inspired the creativity of designers for centuries, and every culture has found a way of accommodating its own relaxation needs. Here are some of today's most popular global seating options:

THE POUF Currently one of the most widely utilized pieces of global furniture, poufs can be seen just about everywhere, from movies and magazines to stylish living rooms. Though usually attributed to Moroccan design traditions, poufs are historically common to Egypt and northern Nigeria as well. Kano, once the leading city of the Hausa empire in Nigeria and a major center of culture and trade, is particularly well known for the quality of its leather poufs. Versatile in both form and function, poufs come in a variety of sizes and shapes. Both square and round poufs serve in various interior settings as seating, tables, or footrests. And since many come in a variety of candy-coated shades, choosing a pouf as one of your seating options can also be an interesting way to add a pop of color to a room.

HAND-CARVED AFRICAN STOOLS Stools are one of the most pervasive furniture traditions among Africa's many cultures. There are literally hundreds of styles to choose from. Hand-carved stools have long been used as ceremonial seating and to indicate the status and power of tribal chiefs and kings. Some of today's most popular coffee and side table designs were first conceived of as seating in African countries, including Bamileke and Senufo stools.

Stools designed by the Bamileke people of Cameroon are fit for royalty. Carved from a single piece of local teum wood and stained with dark shoe polish, the stool is made for the king to sit upon during public ceremonies. The distinctive crisscross pattern is representative of the earth spider, an insect that is used in divination practices among the Bamileke.

In sizes both big and small, Bamileke stools are often used as coffee and side tables in modern interiors. Outside of traditional venues, they are often found in exciting new hues, including white and gold.

Senufo stools are more than just stools; they are one-of-a-kind works of art. The sculptural design of Senufo stools has made them popular pieces for the home. Crafted from a single piece of wood and hand-carved by the Senufo people of Ivory Coast, these stools make great side tables and footrests.

Today, designers from around the world are seeing African wood carvings in a whole new light. Not only are craftsmen reinterpreting traditional African wares, they are also creating new designs based on African concepts. New seating options like the Binta armchair from Swiss designer Philippe Bestenheider are inspired by African wood carvings and Senegalese patchwork fabrics. These innovative takes on traditional furniture are a wonderful way to bring a global feel to your modern space.

THIS PAGE: Look for seating with beautiful hand-carved details to add interest to your space. Bamileke stools can have a variety of uses in your interior. They are great for extra seating and can also be used as side tables. Group several together for a unique display in your living room. OPPOSITE: Update your global finds to fit into modern décor. Designer James Saavedra gave new life to a Bamileke stool by painting it gold for a touch of glamour.

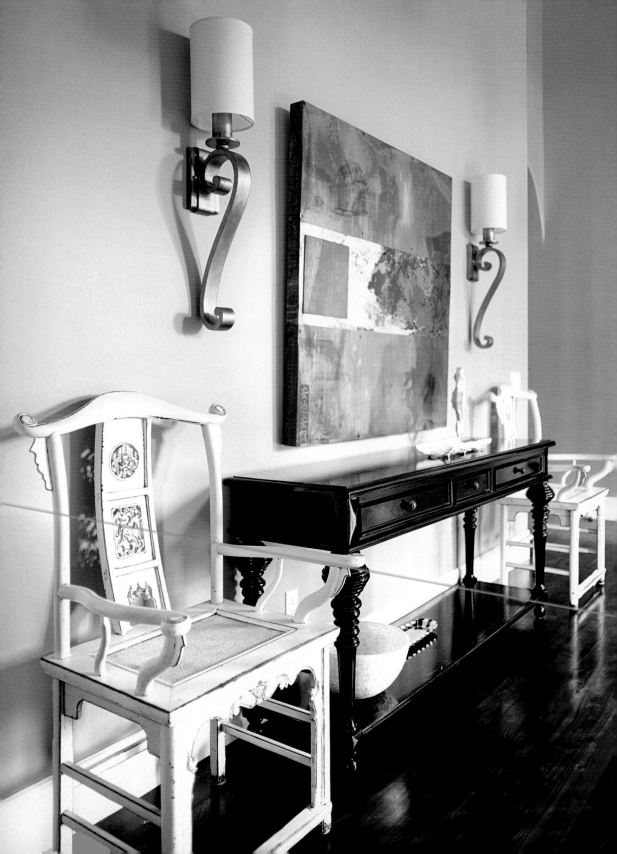

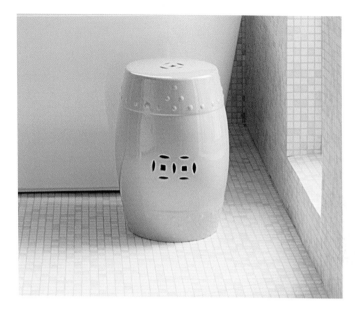

RIGHT: Chinese seating comes in a variety of attention-grabbing shapes and colors. These furnishings make excellent statement pieces in your living and dining areas or even in a bathroom. Bring in garden stools in vivid shades of yellow, red, and blue to add color to a space in the form of side tables and extra seating. OPPOSITE: Classic Chinese armchairs can set your dining room apart. Paint them in neutral shades such as crisp white, or go bold with emerald green or hot pink.

CLASSIC CHINESE SEATING The staying power of Chinese furniture styles is astounding; designs that were first introduced centuries ago remain just as attractive today, inspiring us to constantly find new uses for these ancient pieces.

The classic Chinese garden stool has been around for close to a thousand years. The barrel shape was inspired by natural tree stumps and the large rocks used in cultivating herb and flower gardens in China. Contemporary stools have moved beyond the drum shape, and garden stools can be found in square, spherical, and hexagonal profiles, as well as in a number of finishes from cracked porcelain to iridescent paints. The level of variety to be found in these pieces makes them wonderful furnishing accents that offer a colorful global appeal as well as an interesting sculptural element for your home.

From lacquered Chippendale chairs to carved antiques, Chinese chairs hold centuries of history and depth in their designs. And yet these pieces are finding places in today's homes as side chairs, dining chairs, and accent pieces. The beautiful carved lines of a Qianlong period armchair, a design dating back to the eighteenth century, or the often-reproduced Chippendale chair are traditional with a twist: you can find reproductions painted in bright, colorful tones, including bright whites that make these classically themed pieces feel modern and eclectic.

LEFT: Hand-carved pieces like this beautiful chair from India can bring a rich cultural detail to your room. **OPPOSITE:** An intricately designed bone inlay chair is a treasured piece that speaks to the black-and-white patterned rug in this home office.

INDIAN TREASURE: BONE INLAY SEATING With a rich history that spans North Africa, Persia, China, and India, bone inlay chairs and benches have a history that goes back as far as the sixteenth century, when Mughal princes brought exotic Moorish designs from Africa into India. These pieces, which are intricately adorned with mother-of-pearl or hand-cut camel bone, are exquisitely designed. In dining rooms, living rooms, and spaces that call for additional seating, bone inlay chairs have become a popular option. The sophisticated design of these chairs has the ability to complement contemporary pieces and also looks great when paired with more modern and stream-lined furnishings.

TABLES

From the Bamileke stools that are now utilized as coffee tables and side tables to traditional Ethiopian baskets that double as eating trays, traditional global tables often serve dual purposes. The ability of these pieces to bring a sense of old-world functionality to more aesthetically driven modern spaces means they not only are great design pieces but can also help solve some of the issues of living with limited space. The fun of discovering the world of tables is in identifying the creativity and style that functions best for your living environment.

MOROCCAN TEA TABLES You'll know the design of a Moroccan tea table when you come across it. A folding wooden base topped with a heavy metal tray filled with Islamic geometric patterns and with poufs and pillows surrounding it, this table is the perfect way to dine in Moroccan style. It is also a fantastic option when looking for an

Coffee tables and side tables imported from around the globe can add sophistication to your space. Look for out-of-the-ordinary ottomans, trays, and hand-crafted pieces.

LEFT: A small accent table in the form of an African drum stool is an inventive way to add cultural style to your space. OPPOSITE: Teak tables fit beautifully into an interior when you mix them with modern elements. Surround a rustic dining table with contemporary pieces, such as these Saarinen "Tulip" chairs in bright white, to transform a space from ultrarustic to sleek and modern.

unconventional coffee table. These tables are well suited for small spaces because they can be folded and put away when extra room is needed. You can also find modern-day iterations of these iconic tables at large retail chains like Pottery Barn.

ETHIOPIAN MESOBS The Ethiopian basket table, or mesob, is a colorfully woven lidded basket used for serving traditional Ethiopian meals. The top of the mesob is simply lifted off, and a platter is placed in the center of the basket table for a unique dining experience. Basket tables such as these can often be found at Ethiopian restaurants. The real beauty in these basket tables is the multiple functions they can serve. They can be used as tables at outdoor parties, and also as storage and utility baskets to organize household items. Mesobs are the perfect option for smaller interiors where space is at a premium and furniture has to perform more than one job.

INDONESIAN TEAK A popular wood because of its beautiful grain, texture, and durability, Indonesian teak can stand up to weather and pests and is easily treated with oil, varnish, and even soap and water, making it the perfect material for both indoor and outdoor furnishings. The solid planks of the handcrafted wood complement both modern and traditional designs because of their warm patina, which looks beautiful when paired with classic dining chairs or more modern pieces.

Sourcing Furniture and Accessories

You can source global objects from a variety of places, whether on your travels or from local stores.

- Our best advice is to get out there, travel, and discover pieces that you love while visiting a new place. Search out the local trade, and meet the artisans who create these works. Not only will the pieces carry the culture and history of the place, they'll also keep the special memories of your international adventures.

- If shopping the globe firsthand isn't an option, you don't need a passport to find furniture and accessories from around the world. Look for stores and boutiques that import items from other countries. Many of these stores have knowledgeable owners who do the traveling for you, making worldwide connections to find the most exotic pieces to put on display. They can usually tell you the history and background of a piece and may even have information on appropriate authentication if you are looking to add to a serious collection.

- Many stores offer reproductions of items like Chinese Chippendale chairs and Bamileke stools. These items can be purchased at a fraction of the cost of the real thing. The craftsmanship may not be quite the same, but if you are simply looking for a piece that helps your room achieve a global look, these reproduction pieces will do the trick.

Mixing Objects

In bringing together various global pieces from different cultures, look at how items relate to one another. Play with objects that have both modern and traditional details to create an interesting juxtaposition. For instance, pairing slick Italian dining chairs with a rough-hewn teak table will create a unique dining area.

Identify global furniture and accessories that fit within your room's established color palette. While the lines and shapes of these pieces may be distinctly different from those of the modern furnishings in your space, a shared color palette will help these various pieces fit together like pieces of a puzzle.

While you may want to showcase a mix of global pieces for an eclectic look, there is also value in having one major statement piece. A singular piece like a Cameroonian juju hat or an oversized mask may be the only element you need to infuse your room with all the global style it needs.

A hand-carved door was brought home by these homeowners during their travels to Tibet. They used it to create a stunning entryway to their sleek home office.

Accessories

WOOD CARVINGS

When traveling to places where wood carving is an enduring part of the traditional culture, like Africa and India, look for hand-carved masks, statues, and figurines, which can add texture and a rough-hewn, lived-in feel to your space. Hand-carved ebony and wooden statues can be displayed on shelving, while larger sculptures can take center stage in an entryway or in the living room. Carved objects, like wooden bowls, work well as part of a global collection, and masks are beautiful pieces for adorning your walls.

The most important thing when selecting wood carvings is to identify pieces that speak to you and that have authenticity. While you might find many pseudo-African and -Indian wood carvings in local knockoff shops, conduct a deeper search and look for stores that import items from the objects' country

ABOVE: Wood carvings can be placed throughout your interior. Designer Anna Powers set a pair of hand-carved Tibetan statues in the entryway of her Philadelphia home to welcome guests. A wood carving of an African man is a find from eBay and now lives on this shelf as a creative and one-of-a-kind bookend.
OPPOSITE: To highlight collected carved objects and pieces from your travels, display them on custom shelving.

of origin and whose store owners or managers can tell you the history of a specific piece. And if you find yourself traveling in another country, don't miss the opportunity to purchase these pieces directly from the artisans who actually create them. During our honeymoon in Jamaica, we came across a vendor who produced the most beautiful hand-carved masks. We purchased a piece immediately, but our favorite part was sitting and talking with the artist about the meaning behind the mask, as well as learning more about the man who created it. The opportunity to speak directly with the artisan can be invaluable. You can use the piece you buy as the basis for a larger collection and as a reminder of your time abroad.

RIGHT: A Cameroonian juju hat in a neutral shade can have a striking impact. The feathered headdress adds an unexpected detail to this stone wall. OPPOSITE: A hot-pink juju hat adds a bright pop of color, texture, and a fun global element.

CAMEROONIAN JUJU HATS

The Cameroonian juju hat is one of our favorite global accessories to decorate with. Originally worn by tribal chiefs and dignitaries in the kingdoms of Cameroon, juju hats feature feathers beautifully woven onto a raffia base. In an array of colors that range from deep purple to magenta, red, creamy white, and even jet black, juju hats have the ability to add both color and texture to a space. Whether hung over a mantel or set just off-center, the juju hat is an accessory that commands attention. Try hanging a single hat on the wall for a bright pop of color, or mix three or four hats to create some original wall art. To get started decorating with this striking headwear, all you need to do is pick your favorite colors in varying sizes for your own Cameroonian statement piece.

Thomas Day: Furniture Inspired by America and Beyond

There is nothing more beautiful than a handcrafted piece of furniture. Pieces that have been lovingly made over time with careful precision offer the most classic designs and never go out of style. Many times, we think of global furnishings in terms of Danish Modern design or the sleek silhouettes of Italian pieces. But there are also those made right in our own backyard that are just as intriguing and that have a bit of a global history to them as well.

One interesting tale is the story of furniture maker Thomas Day. A free African American living in North Carolina in the days before the Civil War, Day became one of the South's most sought-after craftsmen. Born in 1801 to free African American parents, Day learned the trade of a cabinetmaker from his father, who was himself a respected artisan. Entering into the furniture business with his older brother, Day specialized in creating custom pieces. He was commissioned to furnish the interior woodwork for one of the original buildings at the University of North Carolina at Chapel Hill. The pews he built still stand in the Milton Presbyterian Church, which he attended. And his craftsmanship was known across the South, a reputation that garnered numerous requests from wealthy clients, including two North Carolina governors.

Day was particularly famous for his architectural flourishes. While some have perceived an African influence in the curved forms that he employed, Day's designs are generally believed to show a mix of influences, making them uniquely American. His work was influenced by classical European design reflecting Gothic, Greek Revival, and rococo styling.

At the height of his success, Day owned the largest furniture business in North Carolina. Today, the expansive Union Tavern, which Day purchased in 1848 to serve as his home and workshop, is preserved as a historical landmark and museum. Thomas Day works can also be seen at the North Carolina Museum of History. And many wealthy homes across the South still hold the legacy of an African American man who is remembered as one of the founding fathers of the North Carolina furniture industry.

American-Made Is Also Global

We absolutely love sourcing and using furnishings from around the world, but we have a great appreciation for American furniture design as well. A few years ago we visited the High Point Market in High Point, North Carolina, to see what has been dubbed "the furniture capital of the world" in action. This international market hosts thousands of attendees from all over the globe, proving that American furnishings are also a large player in an international market. There are still American companies that create beautiful furniture design with dedication to traditional methods and fine craftsmanship. These pieces should not be overlooked but should be considered among the rich and beautiful pieces that will make your home a globe-trotting story of the worldwide marketplace in which we all live.

This tray was bought on a trip to the African continent and is displayed in the home's kitchen.

PART TWO

MODERN SOULFUL HOMES

The soulful home is a unique one. Like the people who conceive of them, no two are completely alike. The homes collected here combine each of the four elements of AphroChic style to tell stories of artists and designers, musicians, and collectors. All of these spaces are the homeowner's personal statements on who they are and the influences that shape their interiors.

A New York songstress designs an interior where her love of music and iconic images take center stage.

MAIYSHA SIMPSON
BROOKLYN LULLABY
PARK SLOPE, BROOKLYN, NEW YORK

"But where's the place and when's the time," Maiysha Simpson wonders aloud, "for me to live the life that's mine? I wonder if I'll ever make it home?" The question is posed in the song "Wannabe," one of the thirteen tracks that graced this singer's debut album. Full of passion and

longing, the song is a woman's assessment of herself as she catalogs her strengths and flaws and, accepting all of it, wonders if she will ever be the person that she'd hoped in the place that she'd always dreamed of. A familiar question in a city that's hardly ever a buyer's market.

In 2006, when the singer decided to leave Manhattan for Brooklyn, she went to a broker with a list in hand detailing everything that she wanted and needed from her new home. It was a short search. Maiysha fell in love with the very first place she saw: a spacious one-bedroom, ground-floor apartment in one of Park Slope's historic brownstones.

At the top of her list of must-haves was that her new home needed to suit her hectic lifestyle. When she's not recording music or performing, the talented songstress works as a model for the prestigious Ford Models. With both of her careers sending her around the globe and her need to be productive when at home, Maiysha found herself looking for a space that would be as much an office and a studio as an oasis.

PREVIOUS: Because she spends so much time traveling, homeowner Maiysha Simpson created a space that would be her personal sanctuary at home. She designed the ideal refuge in her bedroom, where she surrounds herself with her very own personal affirmation written on the walls. **ABOVE AND OPPOSITE:** The secret behind Maiysha's success with color in her home is that she helps diffuse strong color with neutral furnishings and accessories. A large birch shelving unit, cream side chair, white sofas, and a Mexican Otomí tapestry in white and beige break up the expanse of turquoise and red that forms the foundation of this colorful and energetic interior.

The singer credits her birthplace, Minneapolis, the city that gave us the music of Prince and Sounds of Blackness, for some of the more eclectic and musically focused aspects of her style. In her home office, she features her musical and iconic influences through a collection of black-and-white photographs and prints.

Now, amid the tree-lined streets and historical architecture that characterize her Brooklyn neighborhood, the former Manhattanite has found the perfect environment in which to design a truly melodious space. "It's a beautiful neighborhood full of brownstones, great restaurants, and lots of amenities," she says. The affluent and family-focused area has a reputation of being a bit exclusive, yet Maiysha does not count this sense of separation among her neighborhood's flaws. "I love that the neighborhood is basically its own self-contained universe. It reminds me of the area I grew up in."

Yet even with her current need for peace and quiet, Maiysha has no intention of changing her affinity for urban areas. "I'm definitely a city kid," she admits.

As you enter the singer's home, you can see the eclectic influences come together with bright shades, interesting architectural details, and even a few photos of Prince sprinkled into the mix. One step into the living room and guests will find themselves immediately enveloped in color. Ocean blues in the open-plan living and dining area and red walls in the office grab your attention. While the colors of her rooms invite you in, Maiysha's personal touches beg you to stay. Beautiful photography, musical inspira-

tions, and some of her own DIY projects throughout the space entice you to sit a while and explore what this music maven has up her sleeve when it comes to interior design.

Maiysha wanted to go big with color from the start, using the large palette of her walls to tell her color story. "Wall color became a really exciting tool for me when I was just starting to define who I was and how I wanted to live," she states. "I've allowed my furniture to be the blank canvas, and my walls have become the art." Turquoise walls, redolent of summer seas and island getaways, bring the living and dining rooms together. Neutral-colored furniture, wall moldings in white, and honey-toned shelving, storage, and flooring all complement the walls' bright hue.

The home's turquoise color was a clever solution to a problem created by one of Maiysha's least favorite parts of her apartment, a blue Formica kitchen counter that gave the room a '70s vibe. Now, the Formica disappears within a turquoise backdrop, and the singer's talent for combining bright shades and neutral tones takes center stage. Just like in the living area, birch wood and white furnishings break up the blue and create a nice contrast in this dining area.

The dining room is grounded with glass and chrome in the form of an oversized mirror above the buffet and a glass table that can comfortably sit guests for Maiysha's many impromptu dinner parties. Chrome also accents the kitchen bar, where Bertoia barstools are covered in white sheepskin throws that soften the chairs' industrial design.

While the blue is substantial, Maiysha's dining area displays striking tones of black and white through an amazing gallery of monochrome photography. Covering a wide array of shapes, sizes, and subjects, her collection is the result of many years of acquisition. This long-standing fascination with black-and-white photography began with a few postcards Maiysha received as gifts after first arriving in New York. "I'm especially attracted to black-and-white images of black people," she explains, "so over the years, it became a habit to seek them out and collect them whenever I saw an arresting shot."

At first glance, the collection reveals a series of iconic images featuring important cultural figures of the African Diaspora, from Nelson Mandela to Ella Fitzgerald. But on closer inspection, faces less familiar, yet no less striking, become increasingly present. Mixed in with the array of important figures and pivotal moments are quiet remembrances of family and friends. "For me," says Maiysha, "the subject isn't as important as the image, which is why I integrate family, friends, and unknown subjects with well-known icons. It's all art and all captured moments of humanity. Displaying them as a single collection emphasizes that." Though not universally recognizable, these images are all the more special because of the meaning they bring to this unique assemblage.

Hanging above the dining room is an innovative chandelier that is one of Maiysha's favorite pieces. The geometric design of the wooden light fixture is both a complement and a contrast to the white Art Deco tin ceiling that covers both the living room and the dining room in a similar triangular motif. Using the two together adds pattern to her space in a wonderfully unorthodox way while drawing the eye to the dazzling vista that waits overhead.

Maiysha's love affair with neutrals and blues continues in the living room with a few fun touches. Magenta, silver, and gold accent pillows add excitement to a white sofa and bench while maintaining a peaceful and relaxing tableau. The room also weaves in a bit of romance with pretty feminine details. AphroChic pillows sporting watercolor designs depict women enjoying different aspects of Brooklyn life.

ABOVE: This home is filled with DIY ingenuity. An oversize pendant lamp discovered in a thrift shop was rejuvenated by some easy rewiring done by the homeowner. **LEFT:** Use accessories such as pillows and cushions to express your personal style at home. Here, an AphroChic "Fort Greene" pillow shows off the homeowner's love of Brooklyn. **OPPOSITE:** Among family photos, Maiysha likes to mix in iconic images of those who inspire her. In the home's dining room are pictures of Ella Fitzgerald, Luther Vandross, and Nelson Mandela. The images, though varied and taken by a variety of photographers, come together seamlessly in black and white.

It's the smallest elements that personalize a space, like this bust of Jimi Hendrix, which embodies Maiysha's passions for global design, music, and soul. Vintage pieces, found objects, and items that are bought during travel can be used to add personality and a unique story to your interior.

soundtrack

Songs That Make a Space Croon in Falsetto

When this singer is looking for a little peace and quiet, she puts on these five songs to chill:

1 **"Willing & Able"** —PRINCE

2 **"Sometimes"** —THE NOISETTES

3 **"Feels Like the First Time"** —CORINNE BAILEY RAE

4 **"It Ain't Over ('til It's Over)"** —LENNY KRAVITZ

5 **"Feelings"** —VAN HUNT

While her pillows sit in quiet homage to her beloved city, an unmistakable global influence is apparent throughout Maiysha's interior. An avid traveler, the singer has amassed a collection of global wares that she likes to display in her home. "I try to bring home something I love from every trip. These pieces have so much meaning to me because they remind me of this amazing career I've been able to have." Above the living room bookshelves is another series of black-and-white photos, depicting life in an African village; it was brought back from a trip to Cape Town, accompanied by an antique Coptic cross, which now sits on a side table.

The most stunning piece from Maiysha's time abroad is an embroidered fabric created by the Otomí of Central Mexico. Purchased at a roadside stand during a photo shoot in Tulum, the wall hanging fabric is one of the home's larger patterned statements.

The living room coffee table is a family heirloom passed down from her mother. "I am deeply in love with a lot of items in my home," Maiysha explains, "but hands

down, my propeller coffee table is my favorite. It was one of the first things my mother bought for herself when she became single, and the first thing she gave to me when I moved into my first place. It's a daily reminder of my brilliant mom."

As Maiysha's major passion, music is the central theme of her office. Feeling worlds away from the soothing beach tones of the living room, there's no mistaking that the office is a place for getting things done. As in her other rooms, Maiysha relies on her walls as her main statement pieces, and the walls say that this is no place for taking it easy. This room bursts with energy, driven by bright red tones intended to get the singer's creative juices flowing.

Finding the right color for her work space wasn't easy. Caught between the desire to organically cultivate her creativity and the need to be productive, the artist found that she had some difficult choices to make. "I needed something dynamic and power-ful for my creative space," says Maiysha, "something I couldn't just walk through and ignore." Initially her search for color inspi-

ABOVE: To break up the red in her office, Maiysha continued the white trim from the living room and brought in a white sofa for lounging. Additional pieces of the living room color palette continue to drift in. Turquoise pillows add a much-needed note of relaxation. A cool black-and-white lampshade adds a dash of pattern, and the rest of the room is decorated in what she loves most: music. **OPPOSITE:** In the office, color and art create a soulful space. In the typographic print hanging above the desk are more personal affirmations: THIS IS YOUR LIFE and SHARE YOUR PASSION.

Photos of musical icons such as Nina Simone and
Aretha Franklin provide inspiration while Maiysha's
working.

ration led her to paint the walls in a familiar coral-pink hue that she'd used in earlier homes. "I assumed it would create a 'nurturing' space to work in. Wrong. In a windowless room, the whole effect just ended up feeling . . . womblike."

Maiysha found her solution in the form of an iconic shot of Grace Jones: "Hot, sexy, tomato red was the answer. I love the color so much, I've started wearing it regularly!"

Though the supercharged tones of the office may grab the singer's attention in a way that is more challenging than nurturing, the combination of colors perfectly complements the space where Maiysha marshals her energies, actively dedicating herself to the continual process of refinement that is required of a creative career.

If Maiysha's office is a place for stimulating creativity, her bedroom is a shrine to simplicity. Uncomplicated and refreshing, the color choices in this room are strikingly different from those in the rest of the interior. Here, white walls set the tone of a medi-

tative space, and color emerges sparingly through furniture, textiles, and art. Chinese Chippendale chairs upholstered with hot-pink cushions bring in color as well as a global influence with an Asian vibe. An X-bench at the foot of the bed brings in the same golden hues that are present in the living room, while textiles add a cultural touch.

On the bed, African-inspired patterns adorn the pillows, while a single black pillow that Maiysha made from an Indian sari adds a bit of drama. "I'm very inspired by textiles and imagery, and often re-create pieces I've seen while traveling, or use something I've seen as inspiration for a room or a vignette," she says. "My favorite thing to do is to cover pillows with silk saris, vintage obis, and ikat fabrics. I layer them to maximize the interplay between the patterns and textures. It's a quick-and-easy way to add some exotic flavor."

ABOVE: A vintage phone has been given new life on the bedside table. Vintage photographs, postcards, and other treasures are collected in a nearby box to add personal accents to the bedroom. **LEFT:** Bangles and jewelry create an interesting patterned display. Simply placed on a tray, this ever-growing collection becomes a decorative feature in the room. **OPPOSITE:** The bedroom is filled with cultural touches. On the bed, pillows by Hammocks & High Tea feature an African-inspired print. Maiysha repurposed an Indian black sari, stitching it into a throw pillow for the bed.

Art continues to have an important place in the bedroom. Among family photos and postcards from her travels, typographic art is on display next to the bed. From inspirational prints and a framed message proclaiming her "Queen of Effing Everything," it's clear that Maiysha believes not only that art can say something but just as strongly that saying something is art. And though her admiration for words is clear, she is quick to warn against going too far: "Surrounding yourself with quotes can get corny, so I choose inspirational or humorous pieces, then treat them as art."

Of course, making words work is something that the Grammy-nominated artist does well. "I'm a writer," she confesses, "so I have a long-standing love affair with words, which has evolved into an affinity for typography as well. I've always had at least one piece of text-driven art in my home, whether it be the word YES printed in random sizes and places throughout the apartment or the canvas I had hanging over my bed that said simply: 'Life in here is beautiful.'"

Standing out against the bright white walls is the statement piece of this room: the

LEFT: Displaying jewelry on a corkboard turns your collection into a great decorative accessory while keeping it organized and untangled. **RIGHT:** A Chinese lacquer chair gets a modern makeover with a hot-pink upholstered seat. **OPPOSITE:** Typographic prints are mixed in with photos to create an eye-catching gallery display. Online sites like Society6 and Etsy make it easy to find typographic prints like these for your own collection.

get maiysha's look

Set the tone in your space with bold color choices, a DIY gallery wall, and pieces from time spent traveling around the world.

Create an Iconic Gallery Wall with Black-and-White Photos

A framed collection of black-and-white photography brings an art gallery feel into Maiysha's dining room. Collect black-and-white images of some of your favorite icons. Look for postcards, and even images from books and magazines that you can easily clip out. Place them together among your black-and-white family photos to create a personal gallery wall filled with images of family, friends, and those who inspire you.

Put Your Favorite Shades to Work

To add color to her interior, Maiysha started with paint. The turquoise walls in Legendary Blue by Pratt & Lambert set the tone in the living room and dining area. In the office, an energetic feel was created by covering the walls in Valspar's Cherry on Top. Take a trip to your local paint store, and choose two or three shades that you think will set the tone for your rooms.

Design Your Own Patterned Wallpaper

Maiysha created "wallpaper" with chalkboard paint and simple script. A chalkboard wall can be a perfect backdrop and a patterned piece in your room. Once you apply the paint, have fun with chalk by creating patterns, typographic art, and sketches to add decoration to your space.

Create an Eclectic Global Mix

Pieces from South Africa, Mexico, and Japan come together in Maiysha's home to form a well-traveled collection. Whenever you travel, be sure to pick up a few pieces to bring back home with you. Even a little tchotchke from a local craftsman can help create an interesting global collection at home.

pair of floor-to-ceiling "chalkboard" walls that flank the head of the bed. The crowning artistic achievement of the space, they allow for continual creativity because they can be erased and reinscribed at any time. The chalkboard's current message is, "I'd do it all again," repeated over and over. Besides acting as a sort of wallpaper, the words—and the recursive act of writing them—function as a reaffirmation of the person Maiysha is and the life she's built for herself.

This thought is the driving theme behind Maiysha's entire home, and more than any single element within it, she enjoys how well the whole space conveys that idea. "I'm an entertainer, and my home is built for that. I'm also a person who craves warmth, intimacy, and inspiration, and I've built that into my space as well. More than anything, I love that in my home, almost everywhere I look brings me pleasure."

The singer's Grammy Nominee medallion is featured on a mood board in her office—a reminder of her accomplishments as an artist.

Combining their love of art and midcentury modern design, two artists take an industrial loft from cool to cozy.

ANGELA & LEON BELT
ARTISTS
IN RESIDENCE
NAVY YARD, WASHINGTON, DC

Looking around the Washington, DC, loft of Angela and Leon Belt, it would be easy for guests to believe that they have stumbled into the world's coziest art gallery. And they wouldn't be entirely wrong.

PREVIOUS: These artists showcase their work on floating shelves in the dining area. Each piece is in a distinctive frame but still looks collected, and the floating shelves allow the art to be rotated in and out on a whim.
THIS PAGE: For Angela and Leon, the most interesting part of their home décor is how they've combined styles and furnishings of different periods to create something fresh. In the office, Danish Modern furniture meets industrial chic to form two distinct work spaces.

RIGHT: From the art to the accessories, everything in this home has meaning. A photograph in an ikat frame is a memento from the couple's engagement party. **OPPOSITE:** In Angela's work space, a curvy white chair softens the hard lines of a midcentury modern antique desk that she found online. Her eye for design comes in handy when she sources vintage furniture from sites such as eBay and Craigslist.

This is a space dominated by art, most of which was made by the couple. With a tasteful array of midcentury modern furniture and set against an industrial backdrop, the vast differences in their individual artwork make for a personalized space that speaks to their history as a couple and to their respective visions as artists.

Angela, a visual merchandiser and freelance stylist, prefers to express herself on canvas through mixed media—using various methods and materials in a single piece to capture her audience's attention. A range of techniques including pencil and ink sketches, together with painting, collage, and the very clever use of Scrabble tiles, comprise Angela's style. The tendency toward social commentary and hidden messages in her work has led the artist to label herself a "political abstractionist." For Leon, who works as a videographer and graphic designer, the term "mixed media" is more likely to conjure images of digital photography, video, and computer-animated graphics, the three areas that hold the majority of his artistic interest.

The couple has crafted a space that is equal parts workshop, gallery, and home—built around art, music, and memories, all of the things they are most passionate about. At every turn, this unconventional Washington, DC, loft is a tribute to the works they have created, to the pieces they have collected from fellow artisans and friends, and to fond reminders from their international travels.

It makes perfect sense that art should be such a big part of their design aesthetic. They first noticed each other during an art class at Howard University. Angela recalls, "When I first met Leon, I was intimidated by how talented he was, which led me to move my easel next to his so I could work beside him in art class and get some pointers on how to improve my paintings. From there everything just fell into place, and we have been together ever since."

The couple's search for a space with industrial flavor was difficult in Washington, DC, a city known for traditional row homes in a variety of Federalist and Victorian styles. It wasn't until Leon took a job as a videographer shooting a short film near DC's newly rehabilitated waterfront that he discovered the home they had been looking for. The couple's new neighborhood had formerly been a section of the Washington Navy Yard

that had been used to service fleet ships during World War II. The area had been given a massive facelift with once-empty warehouses becoming expansive urban lofts. A public park and water feature rivaling New York City's High Line had also been created. It was an opportunity that neither could resist.

While the outside of Leon and Angela's apartment building showcases the precision of modern architecture, the interior gives center stage to the less orderly interpretations of life offered by art. To complement the collection of paintings, illustrations, and photography that they've personally created, Angela and Leon have incorporated a wide variety of handcrafted furnishings, including their bed and the living room coffee table. Sourcing such pieces from various artisans in open markets like the Brooklyn Flea or DC's Eastern Market has become a habit as they've moved from place to place. Finding accessories

ABOVE: Leon's mandolin rests against the industrial shelving, ready to be played when the mood strikes. **LEFT:** The couple finds fun ways to introduce modern elements among their midcentury pieces, like this new turntable. **OPPOSITE:** After graduating together, the couple went on to live in a number of different cities, collecting furniture, textiles, accessories, and other small tokens from every stop to add to their evolving design style. The result is an eclectic mix of midcentury modern, industrial, and vintage pieces that plays well with their own original artwork.

by repurposing flea market finds or searching out independent artists in their area is the couple's way of ensuring that their home never ends up feeling too mass produced. "It's all about the hunt," Angela confesses. "Finding that one perfect piece that speaks to you is really fun to look for. When I bring home something that's thirty or forty years old, I love that I was able to breathe new life into it."

A look through the entryway reveals all the industrial architectural details that make this space unique. Exposed brick, aluminum piping, hardwood floors, and clean white walls not only take the couple back to their Brooklyn days, they also provide the perfect neutral backdrop for an ever-growing art collection. As you pass through the hall that leads from the front door to the living room, a nine-piece installation created by Angela dominates the long wall, greeting guests. A few feet away in the bedroom, another of her pieces makes a striking fixture over the bed. Exemplifying Angela's preference for mixed media, both works combine paint, pencil sketching, and her signature use of Scrabble

ABOVE LEFT: Art can bring texture into a space. Here, Angela layered tiles and paper in a piece that has a 3D effect. **ABOVE RIGHT:** Create a gallery wall by hanging varying pieces of art or a single collection of related pieces for big impact. **OPPOSITE:** Almost Eames-like in its construction, this black-and-red chair holds a place of honor in the bedroom's reading nook. Like so many pieces in their home, it has a personal story: it was made by Leon's friend during art school. The chair brings home the industrial style and handmade craftsmanship that the couple enjoys.

tiles to either hide messages or defy meaning altogether. The mesmerizing three-dimensional effect that these pieces create never fails to spark questions from first-time visitors. "It's always nice to talk with guests about the work on the walls and why we chose to paint or photograph this or that," Leon observes.

For dramatic infusions of color, pattern, and global-inspired design, Angela used textiles that speak to all three elements. An African-inspired kilim sits atop the bedroom's beige carpet, the navy-blue color breaking up the white and cream in the room. On the bed, a pillow featuring an African Kuba print complements the striped sheets and the oversized floral duvet in a classic palette of gray

Create a patterned mix with bedding. Here, striped sheets, an African Kuba print pillow, and a floral duvet form a beautiful patterned display. Keep the colors cohesive so that various patterns can work together without looking too busy.

soundtrack

Songs That Express an Artsy Vibe

Here are the top five songs Angela and Leon love to play when they entertain friends for an art gathering:

1 "I'm a Lady"
   —SANTIGOLD

2 "Quarter Chicken Dark"
   —GOAT RODEO SESSIONS

3 "Postcards from Italy"
   —BEIRUT

4 "Still Ray"
   —RAPHAEL SAADIQ

5 "Double Trouble"
   —THE ROOTS FEAT.
    MOS DEF

Pastel arrows from the Etsy shop Fletcher and Fox add a colorful display to the bedroom dresser. Angela showcases a collection of white ceramics as works of art. Use small pieces, such as bud vases and bowls, to add color and pattern to a modern space.

and white. A big fan of layering small pops of color into her space, Angela always adds a bright hue, like her orange quilt, which brightens the bedding.

While both Leon and Angela attest to the importance that they attach to bold color in their artwork, bringing color into their apartment is accomplished in small doses. The living room stands out as the apartment's most colorful space. In it, another kilim from Anthropologie brings in a striking kaleidoscope of shades. To ground the varying tones, the couple decided on a streamlined charcoal-gray sectional and a Danish Modern coffee table in teak. The combination makes the living room one of Angela's favorite spaces. "Our living room is large enough for friends to sit and lounge on the sectional while others dig in at the dining room table. I love it."

Over the years, they have learned to treat the design of their home as a collaborative affair, with each partner making their contribution.

LEFT: Angela and Leon love to bring home decorative accessories from their travels. They picked up this colorful London tray on their first trip to England. **RIGHT:** The home is full of interesting vintage items on display, such as this old-fashioned produce scale. **OPPOSITE:** Textiles are used to add color and a bit of whimsy to this masculine living room. A kilim from Anthropologie has a kaleidoscope of hues, which sets up the room's color palette. Bright blue and yellow cushions complement the colorful scheme.

They spend hours together scouring sites like Ebay and Etsy for midcentury modern and handmade pieces. Often they'll end up picking something up from a member of their talented cadre of friends, such as a lounge chair created by Christopher Robbins, a friend Leon met while attending Rhode Island School of Design (RISD).

More handmade and classic furnishings can be found throughout the rest of the interior. In the dining room, a Danish Modern hutch has been repurposed as a storage space. Further defining the couple's dining room style is a cool industrial table made with raw wood and metal legs. Angela says, "In our home I mix lots of styles like Danish Modern and industrial chic with found objects to create a seamlessly unified space. It has really become a great place for parties, and we love the fact that people feel like they can just relax and unwind."

There's so much in this home that keeps these two artists inspired, especially in the room they love most. "The most important space in our home is the office space," Angela remarks. "It's where we both go to work on our independent projects. It seems like we're separated because we're on opposite sides of the room, but it lets us be in our own spaces and really focus on our own projects." This room is filled with a host of pieces that speak to the years that the couple has spent together. On Angela's desk is a set of jars inscribed with the numbers 5-2-9, marking the day that Leon proposed. Near them sits the couple's handmade wedding cake topper—one of the many Etsy finds that Angela used to decorate on their special day. Meanwhile, a pair of abstract paintings composed by Leon during their time at the University of California, Berkeley, hangs over a bookshelf that the two purchased at GoodWood, a vintage and antiques store in DC.

In a space both decorated and defined by the work of the people who occupy it, it is amazing to realize that what makes their space a home is that every piece in it—whether created by the couple or not—

While the dining area sports a neutral color palette, accessories that have been collected during international shopping trips add bold hues to the space. A set of blue placemats is a beautiful pop of color for the table, and a tea container in green and black brings more color to the kitchen.

Just like in the home office, the lines of this industrial dining table are softened by curvy white dining chairs. Go bold and mix styles like modern and industrial or vintage and contemporary to create spaces that are varied and interesting.

get angela and leon's look

Give a stark, modern space warmth by bringing home meaningful works of art and layers of color, pattern, and cultural design.

Let Your Own Art Take Center Stage

As artists, Angela and Leon made their art collection central to the design of the home. Follow their lead by framing your favorite travel photographs and homemade art on your walls. And if art isn't a talent that runs in your family, hang an array of prints from your favorite artist or Etsy shop that shows off your personality.

Layer in Small Doses of Color

With the current preference for neutral-toned walls and hardwood floors, some modern lofts may not offer lots of opportunity for color, so use textiles to layer it in. Angela brought in layers of orange and blue in the bedroom to break up the gray-and-white color scheme and to give the space a much needed pop of color. Pieces like a multicolored rug or a jewel-toned bedspread are great for giving a shot of color to an otherwise neutral space.

Play with Pattern

Stripes, florals, and cultural prints can all come together without clashing when unified by a similar color palette. Angela and Leon chose gray-and-white linens in a number of patterns for a unique bedding display. Discover your favorite patterns in one or two shades that you love, and create an eclectic mix that will add excitement to your space.

Go Global with Textiles

Whether it's kilims, dhurries, or Berbers, international rugs can be a great way to add global style to your interior. Like Angela and Leon, visit shops such as Anthropologie and West Elm to discover global-inspired textiles that will complement the modern vibe of your interior.

At every turn in this home there are pieces that tell Angela and Leon's personal story. On the bookshelf in their office, their wedding cake topper, custom-made by a Los Angeles artist, sits atop a stack of books. Tell your story with meaningful pieces of art, collections, and items from your travels.

is a memory. In every corner of the apartment there is something that tells Angela and Leon's story. What makes it special is that so many of those moments have been recorded with their own hands, whether in the paintings that remind them of their first class together at Howard or their most recent projects. The attention that Leon and Angela have paid to surrounding themselves with meaningful pieces is what takes this ultramodern loft and transforms it into a cozy and inviting home. "I feel the most at home when I look around and see all the pictures of us, our work, and the found objects from places we've traveled," Angela tells us. "It's where we go to relax. Our home represents a timeline of our relationship and where we have been as a couple."

With a love of furniture, fashion, and global design, two women have created a soulful home full of personal touches in their up-and-coming Brooklyn neighborhood.

TARA BETHEA & BOA
A SOULFUL ABODE
OCEAN HILL, BROOKLYN, NEW YORK

It takes more than good design to make a home. Expertly blended colors and hand-picked furniture can fill a space, but a home takes something more, a vibe: a feeling you experience from the moment you walk in. In a word, the very best homes have soul, and it can transform an ordinary space into a place of sanctuary and inspiration.

One such transformation has taken place in Ocean Hill, near Brooklyn's Bedford-Stuyvesant neighborhood, where Tara Bethea and her partner, BOA, have filled every inch of their space with objects and furnishings that tell of who they are and where they have been, and that perfectly reflect the life they are building together.

Tara first spotted their condo when it was up for sale in 2010. She showed it to BOA, and the two were immediately attracted to the area. Inside, the floor plan was open,

PREVIOUS PAGE: Tara and BOA started with a beautiful base of warm, neutral colors to create a cozy vibe for their interior. **THIS PAGE:** Tara and BOA decorated their home with meaningful objects. Upon entering, you immediately get a sense of the things that are important to them and the moments they've shared.

and the walls were bare. The condo was a totally clean slate, the ideal canvas for two very design-minded residents.

For BOA, a native of Saint John in the US Virgin Islands, Ocean Hill has proved the right area to find some small reminders of home—particularly among the many West Indian restaurants that occupy the streets near her home.

Several elements of the home's décor are culled from memories of her childhood. "I keep a shell collection," she admits. "I grew up mostly outdoors in a tropical environment amidst a wide variety of foliage. Since then I've brought back shells from every beach I've ever been to around the world."

A furniture designer and entrepreneur, BOA created the floor plan, and she and Tara worked together to fill the space with furniture. "I already had a huge collection," BOA says, "so I chose all of the major furniture." Tara contributed several pieces of her own, drawn from an assortment of pieces bought during her travels and collected in past living spaces. Together, they

ABOVE: To showcase their collection of hand-carved masks, the couple decided to create a gallery wall. While many people think of framed artwork for gallery walls, masks, baskets, and other collected pieces make wonderful global-style installations. **LEFT:** Tara and BOA placed Buddha statues throughout the home in recognition of their beliefs.

RIGHT: This Cherner chair sitting beside an I-ching statue from Bali is the best example of how expert Tara and BOA are at mixing modern and cultural pieces. **OPPOSITE:** The apartment was designed with comfort in mind. Just to the left of the front door, you enter the couple's bedroom, which is enveloped in a black-and-red color palette. The saturated black hues contribute to the room's coziness.

decided on a design that boasted a mix of modern furnishings, warm neutral tones, and cultural touches that evoked their creativity, spirituality, and shared desire to experience life all over the world.

One of the bigger points of compromise in decorating their home was defining its color story. "My previous apartment was a riot of bright colors," says BOA. "After the experience of living with so much color, I really wanted a neutral palette in our new home." Tara is also a fan of big, colorful statements but wasn't quite as ready to let go of her passion for vibrant spaces. "Tara loves to bring in new things that help to break up my parade of taupes and organics," BOA explains.

It doesn't take long to notice a recurring color theme seen throughout the home. Here, dark walls take center stage, with splashes of color from textiles and accessories. In the bedroom, black wallpaper with a flocked pattern creates a dramatic feature wall. Meanwhile, a warm cocoa shade covers both of the adjacent walls, giving the sun-splashed room an irresistible, cozy feel. The bedroom furniture picks up the brown

of the walls, while a tall wrought iron candleholder stands guard near the windows, a perfect match to the black of the feature wall. With bits of red added in through the bedding, the black-and-brown color palette creates the perfect environment in which to wake up in the morning or drift away at the end of a long day. In the living room and dining area, deep brown walls are broken up with pops of white, such as the Panton chairs that surround the dining room table.

For bright tones, the couple layered shades of red and orange throughout the condo. In the office, a slick red desk and shelving unit from IKEA add color, while black-and-white wallpaper in a tree motif accents the desk area. The final pops of color in the office come by way of a collection of orange, coral, and red sari cushions, matched with a pouf that Tara bought at the Brooklyn Flea. The vibrant cushion mixes orange with black and white, tying in every element of the room's palette.

For Tara, the fun of living with a furniture designer is that she can create beautiful one-of-a-kind pieces to meet the specific

ABOVE: To soften the dark walls in the home office, colorful accessories and an array of feminine pieces have been brought into the space. A cherry-red desk, multicolored floral pouf, and scrolled clock break up the room's neutral base. **OPPOSITE:** A collection of jewel-toned Indian sari pillows lines a loveseat made by Thomas Jameson. Cushions like these are a great way to bring color and culture into a small space. Layer them on a sofa in a number of shades to create a colorful statement.

needs of the home. BOA designed a stunning armoire for the living room made from a mix of Kirei board, with sides covered in an orange lacquer. Cleverly carved openings serve as handles for accessing each compartment. When closed, the slots align to suggest the shape of a Buddhist swastika, a symbol of good fortune and eternity. Topped in this home with an image of the Buddha, the armoire becomes more than a storage space, speaking directly to these homeowners' deeply held beliefs in a piece made especially for them.

The armoire is not the only example of BOA's talent to grace the home that she and Tara share. The condo is inhabited by a number of her original designs, which work together to give the entire space a bespoke feel. "I designed a polished steel mirror for the entry," reveals BOA, "as well as the sliding Macassar ebony door in the bedroom, the media cabinet and the custom wall-mounted cabinet above it in the living room, and the armoire with Kirei board doors."

Several of the designs BOA includes in her home décor are also available for purchase through her company, Object Interiors. Others she keeps just for Tara and herself to enjoy.

Their love of pattern in furniture pieces, on textile accessories, and especially on walls can be seen throughout the space. The couple is fond of using wallpaper to add pattern, and they never miss an opportunity. BOA transformed "the IKEA dresser from hell," as she likes to call it, into a unique focal point in the bedroom

ABOVE: One example of a design that BOA keeps "in-house" is the Macassar ebony sliding door that opens into the bedroom. **LEFT:** Among BOA's custom pieces is a beautiful armoire she designed. **OPPOSITE:** In the living room, the Coup d'Grace media cabinet and wall shelf blend BOA's love of natural materials, such as bamboo, with Tara's love of color, which can be seen in the bold pop of orange in the shelving unit's interior lining.

by wrapping it in a favorite wallpaper pattern from Ferm Living. Its cream-and-black design is a nice complement to the bedroom's black feature wall. Wallpaper even enlivens the kitchen, where a three-dimensional branch pattern covers the bar. The specially cut 3D wall covering, which BOA applied by hand, creates an eye-catching conversation starter.

The final layer in this soulful home is the many items that the couple has collected while traveling. "Every time I look at something it reminds me of a trip," says BOA. A collection of hand-carved masks from trips to Gabon, Benin, Costa Rica, and Cameroon is ever growing, taking center stage on the couple's living room wall. For them, it's a great way to showcase the global collection they have built over time.

Many of the couple's travel itineraries reflect their philosophical affinity for Buddhist teachings. Frequent trips to Southeast Asia provide dual opportunities for sourcing

ABOVE: In addition to many of the custom pieces in their home, the couple loves to tackle DIY projects to personalize pieces they've bought. In the bedroom, an IKEA dresser is customized with a favorite wallpaper pattern. **OPPOSITE:** They added 3D wall coverings to the kitchen island for a textured look. The webbed pattern turns an ordinary island into one of the room's many focal points.

products for BOA's import business and for visiting some of the world's most breath-taking temples. At home, BOA, a student of Tibetan Buddhism, and Tara, who follows the Japanese Soka Gakkai school, agree that the aura of relaxation that permeates their abode is due to their practice of punctuating their space with images of the Buddha. "I find the image [of the Buddha] uniquely calming, so I surround myself with as many of them as possible," BOA says.

Out of an empty and ordinary condo, two design-minded people have created a space that looks and feels as well traveled, spiritual, and artistic as they are themselves.

A SOULFUL ABODE 201

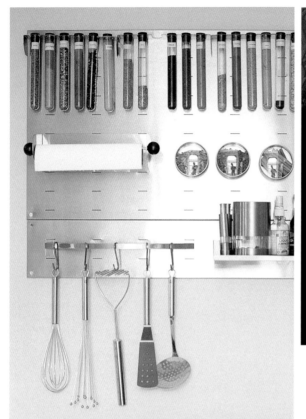

CLOCKWISE: A stainless steel spice rack adds a cool modern element to the kitchen. Orchids sit on the couple's bedside table for a soft, feminine feel. A collection of books in a home office is another way to bring color into the space.

soundtrack

The Sound of a Soulful Abode

Here are four of BOA and Tara's favorite songs for a relaxed vibe:

1 "Comes to Light"
—JILL SCOTT

2 "Night Nurse"
—GREGORY ISAACS

3 "Mas Que Nada"
—MIRIAM MAKEBA

4 "Lovers Rock"
—SADE

The couple used Ferm Living's "Branch" wallpaper to create a statement wall behind their cherry-red desk in the home office. Window panels in gray and white from IKEA add more pattern as light streams into the room.

In the process, they have made a home that is as open and inviting to everyone who enters as it is to the homeowners themselves.

With elements speaking to everything from a childhood in the Virgin Islands to adulthoods spent exploring the holy places of Asia, every inch of BOA and Tara's condo is filled with the thoughts, ideas, and memories that make them who they are, both as individuals and together creating the kind of personal story that fills a home with soul.

Use global objects in unexpected ways to add both functionality and beauty to your home. Instead of a traditional bookshelf, the couple turned a bamboo ladder from Thailand into a piece for displaying magazines in the bedroom.

get boa and tara's look

Create your very own soulful abode with a warm color palette, custom pieces, and global art and accessories that tell your story.

Layer Warm Tones

Rich chocolate browns, charcoal grays, and wood tones can all provide an enveloping effect when used on walls. In a small room, don't be afraid to use dark tones on the wall, especially black. You can use a variety of warm shades to tone down the dark hues and turn a small space into an intimate retreat.

Add Pattern with Wallpaper

This couple loves Ferm Living and used this modern design company's wallpaper to add strong doses of pattern to the rooms in their home. Wallpaper can be used to transform an entire space, or, applied to a single item, it can turn an ordinary piece of furniture into the focal point of your room. Paper can easily be purchased by the roll at online retailers and is great for an afternoon DIY project anywhere you want to create a dramatic effect.

Collect Masks for a Global Display

Avid travelers, BOA and Tara have picked up a lot of items on their journeys and have found unique ways to display them at home. For a collection of masks from various countries, group them together on a wall to create a unique curated collection. Additional pieces can be added over time and will create an eye-catching gallery-style wall in your home.

Feature Your Favorite Artists

Frida Kahlo prints appear throughout the interior of BOA and Tara's home, from a set of small paintings in the bedroom to Frida magnets on the refrigerator. For a budget-friendly way to display works from your favorite artist, put prints together with inexpensive pieces like postcards that represent signature moments in the artist's career.

A rug designer turns a home in need of some TLC into a personal haven through a stylish indulgence in Caribbean-inspired hues, African art, and her own personal designs.

MALENE BARNETT
ISLAND IN THE CITY
BEDFORD-STUYVESANT, BROOKLYN, NEW YORK

It's not every day that someone gets to renovate their own two-story Queen Anne–style townhouse in Brooklyn. For many of us, the thought is just a dream. But for New York rug designer Malene Barnett, it took a few of the right opportunities and a lot of commitment to make her dream come true. In 2008, the native of

Norwalk, Connecticut, bought her very first home, becoming an official New Yorker in the process. She began looking in the area after hearing from a friend that there were homes for sale on a picturesque, tree-lined street in Brooklyn. "I really wasn't looking at the time, but I was open to looking at the space, thinking that I could possibly call it home one day." Once she entered the residence, she found a property in serious need of some tender loving care. Despite its condition, Malene, who studied textile design at the Fashion Institute of Technology (FIT) in Manhattan, saw a chance to put her artistry and ingenuity as a designer to the test.

The result was a two-year project of turning a house that was nearly forgotten into her dream home.

The interior of the large two-bedroom home became a huge canvas for all of Malene's artistic flair. She had years of experience working creatively within the textile industry: first, as the design director for Afritex; and later as an in-house designer for

PREVIOUS: Each room in this home has its own color palette. For Malene, the trick was in narrowing down her color choices to soft shades, like green and blue, to conjure the feeling of ease and comfort in each space. LEFT: The home is filled with sculptures, textiles, and original art. Malene's close friend GA Gardner made the beautiful green collage that hangs in the entryway. RIGHT: Malene had custom handles created for the doors throughout the home as a way to bring small African-inspired touches into her décor.

As you enter the front door, you are greeted by tall African statues that Malene discovered at the Harlem Flea Market. For Malene, bringing culture into her space has a spiritual significance, and in each room some aspect of the African Diaspora is represented.

Nourison Rugs. After so much time spent designing for other companies, Malene felt that it was time to pursue her own vision. In the summer of 2008, the same year in which she closed the deal on her house, Malene decided to step out on her own and developed her self-titled company, Malene B.

"I decided to focus on my passion for carpet design," Malene says. "I wanted to create products that would merge my artistic background with my passion for global travel. Most of all, I wanted to create a company that not only produced great carpet designs but would also inspire others to experience the world through a unique art form that we don't usually think about." The same passion that Malene feels for her rug designs has gone into completing her home as she has worked to craft a modern interior that is bold, colorful, and globally inspired.

Color is the key to every room that Malene has created in this home. "I love

In the home office, a colorful mood board contains inspiration for new projects. Colorways, patterns, new designs, and concepts are all pinned to the board to assist this rug designer with her design process.

color because I'm a colorful person," she explains simply, but there's so much more to it than that. Like every element Malene has brought into her space, the various colors that decorate her rooms, covering the walls and even the floors, are carefully calculated to express her personality, her artistry, and her cultural heritage. Malene confesses that a return to her ancestral home in the Caribbean has always been her ultimate fantasy, and the hues she uses in her interior are intended to evoke a tranquil island paradise reminiscent of the designer's African-Caribbean roots.

While many designers may tell you that blue does not work best in the kitchen because of the cool tone, Malene was focused on creating an oasis that runs through every room of the interior. For that, color is a necessity. "I used the colored walls and floor as the foundation, then added furniture and accessories," Malene says, revealing her secret for narrowing the field when it comes to choosing the right pieces to fill in an interior. "Knowing that the walls and floors are the same color makes decorating easy."

ABOVE AND LEFT: Malene loves to bring culture into her space through fabrics, furniture, and accessories. Beautiful African textiles bought during her travels and her own culturally inspired rugs are a constant source of cultural inspiration.

Before layering accessories into the kitchen, Malene decided on a shade that would be a soft backdrop to the kitchen's bright-white lacquer cabinets and stainless steel appliances. "My teal-stained wood floors . . ." she muses, "I love how the colored floors make you feel as if you are walking on water."

In the dining area, which is part of the kitchen's open-plan design, Malene added another essential element to her space: one-of-a-kind built-in shelving nooks carved out of a long wall overlooking the dining table. Malene's nooks serve as a gallery to some fascinating artwork. The first collection of small statuary we've ever seen included in a kitchen design, Malene's pieces are great conversation starters for guests in the dining

THIS PAGE: In the kitchen, a series of artistic vignettes are on display. Malene showcases African wood carvings, paintings, and ceramics to express her love of cultural arts and handcrafts. OPPOSITE: The calming colors in the kitchen are inspired by the homeowner's love of the Caribbean. While she dreams of a tropical beach house, she has made every effort to bring the feel of the islands into her home.

area, with each one holding special memories for the designer. "My mini art gallery in the kitchen showcases some of my favorite fine arts and crafts," she says. "I purchased most of these pieces during my travels around the world. Each one has a unique story that allows me to reminisce about my trips abroad."

The teal shade that blankets the kitchen continues into the living room. Malene loves to entertain, and her spacious living room is the perfect environment for large-scale, standing-room-only partying. The décor in this room is accentuated by original paintings by Malene's friend GA Gardner. Included among them is a gorgeous mixed-media portrait depicting the image and biography of author Zora Neale Hurston. And the layout of the room never fails to highlight its biggest conversation pieces: Malene's latest rug designs.

On the living room floor, Malene's "Calabash" rug adds to the blue-toned theme of the room. The piece is inspired by the

ABOVE: With an expansive textile collection, Malene features patterned pieces of fabric throughout her home. An African print takes center stage in one of the kitchen's built-ins, and Kuba-print fabric is the slipcover for a dining room chair. **OPPOSITE:** The custom shelving built into the wall is an unconventional concept for a kitchen and breakfast room, and a nice surprise in a home where art and original design are such a big part of the aesthetic.

organic shape of the calabash fruit, which is believed to have originated in various parts of Africa. The design offers a way for Malene to bring both pattern and cultural design into the space. "Pattern can be found everywhere," she says, "and one should not live without color or pattern. The inspiration for my own patterns comes from visiting different places like Dakar, Mumbai, and Kuala Lumpur as well as from my African-Caribbean heritage. Every culture has a different way of looking at things that can be expressed through its patterns."

The blue on blue color palette of the living room changes to a mix of teal and grassy

In the living room, soft colors, plush seating, an open layout, and a romantic fireplace make it a great spot for entertaining. In fact, Malene has hosted some of Brooklyn's most innovative African American designers in this space.

green in the adjacent sitting room. The change in palette is captured in another of Malene's original carpets, called "Moorea," a sunburst design based on the shape of Tahitian palm fronds. The sitting area also includes some striking elements that touch on Malene's global roots. A collection of African sculptures adorns her credenza. Her sculpture collection can be seen throughout the space, the most interesting pieces being the group of four five-foot-tall West African wood carvings that greet guests as they come through the front door. Similar statues are also found in an alcove carved into the wall of the stairway and even appear as the handles on the front door.

For Malene, these pieces add layers of meaning to her space, speaking to the long history that influences both her understanding of herself and her perspective on those who went before her. "Every day, I'm grateful to have a space where I can showcase my cultural heritage, feel protected, and be inspired by my ancestors," Malene explains. "I have a spiritual connection to all of my pieces, especially my collection of Senufo rhythm beaters; they both welcome guests and protect my home. My collection of African art is a mix of traditional and contemporary designs: it truly reflects the things that I really love."

Beautifully carved wooden seating and masks are a nod to Malene's heritage.

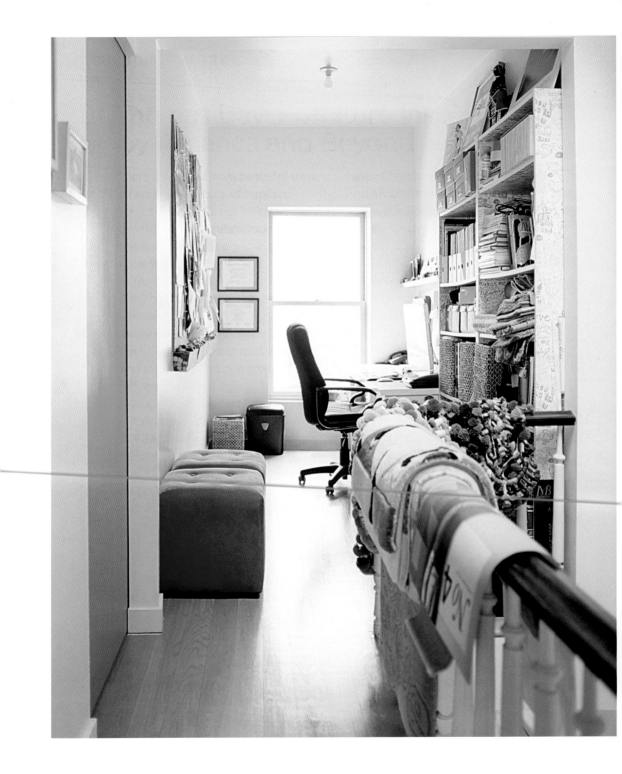

RIGHT: In the home's staircase another unique built-in showcases a collection of African sculptures. Malene painted the walls in a peachy hue to transition from the staircase directly into the home's colorful office. **OPPOSITE:** In the office, Malene's bookshelf carries a densely packed library of books on design, travel, and the history and culture of the African Diaspora. It's all part of the ever-evolving field of stimulation that keeps this designer motivated.

Up a flight of stairs that lead to the upper levels of Malene's home, the color story undergoes another change. The tranquil tones of blue and green fall away, and emerging peach hues cover the walls that accompany guests up and into the home office. The tone is bright and sunny, a dramatic shift from the sea tones of the first floor, yet in perfect harmony with the home's continuing island theme. "It's the perfect color for getting work done," Malene offers. The office also happens to be one of the only areas in the house where the walls and floors do not share the same color. Instead, the blue of the living room floor travels up the stairs and into the office—a rolling sea beneath the sunny sky intimated by the color of the walls. Mood boards and rug samples add their own bright pops of color to the work space. Concepts for projects old and new and prototypes in various stages of completion sit on the desk and hang clustered together on the wall.

A beautiful tapestry adds subtle pattern to the bedroom and complements the light-purple hue that extends from the walls to the floors. The vivid textile behind the bed serves as both a pop of colorful art and a one-of-a-kind headboard.

In Malene's bedroom, the peach tones of the office transition into lighter shades of lilac with an effect similar to watching a sunset fade gently into dusk. Here, again, the walls and floors have been painted the same color: "I found stained-wood flooring for each room and later had the paint custom-mixed so the walls would match," Malene explains. The effect is quite soothing and sets the tone for the tranquil retreat that this bedroom is designed to be. Cultural pieces mixed into the décor help to define the identity of this room as well. An embroidered tapestry makes a creative headboard for the bed, and a gorgeous hand-carved African stool is used as a side table in the room.

Among the bedroom's most interesting features are the double doors that lead into the expansive, spalike bathroom. Our attention was immediately captured by the unique door handles. Reminiscent of the front door, these beautifully sculpted Buddha handles fit nicely against the cool lilac backdrop, completing the Zen-like stillness of the bedroom.

The inside of the bathroom is a different story. Hot pink lines the inside of the bathroom door. The color transition is striking, as is Malene's ingenuity. Even in the bathroom, she comes up with unique and interesting ways to integrate global style. The bathroom is dotted with Asian elements. A Chinese cabinet has been turned into a double sink. And for a bright pop of color, Malene brought in a sunny yellow Chinese garden stool. Through her masterful use of color, Malene has succeeded in creating a home that both conveys and cultivates her personality. With a room to suit every mood, each hue has clearly been chosen with loving care, and each element has been thoughtfully applied to complement

LEFT: Figurative art is on display in the bedroom. A ceramic bust adds a sculptural detail to the dresser. **RIGHT:** On the doors of the en suite bathroom, cast Buddha heads have been turned into stunning door handles.

CLOCKWISE: A Dogon stool adds another cultural element to the home's bedroom. Color and pattern come together beautifully in this small step stool in the home's dressing room. A vintage basket used for storage adds texture to the space.

soundtrack

Five Songs for a Caribbean Groove

Malene's Caribbean-style home keeps her refreshed and motivated all day: "My playlist is a mix of international music, R&B, and pop. It keeps me inspired." Her top five songs for inspiration are:

1 "Zimbabwe"
—BOB MARLEY

2 "Beussem"
—DOBET GNAHORÉ

3 "Moor Ndaje"
—YOUSSOU N'DOUR

4 "The Truth"
—INDIA.ARIE

5 "This Is My World"
—DARIUS RUCKER

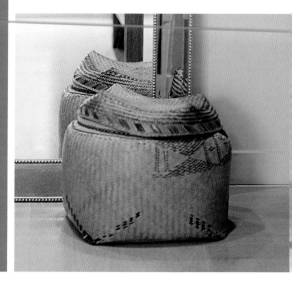

the many color transitions, lending cultural and emotional depth to each space. In Brooklyn's Bed-Stuy neighborhood, Malene Barnett has created another world. Full of color, culture, and identity, it's a space where she can work, create, and then sit back and enjoy the fruits of her labor. While Malene may not have a home in the Caribbean just yet, creating her own personal island in the heart of Brooklyn has proved to be the next best thing.

Hot-pink doors and a yellow Chinese garden stool are all the color that's needed in this calming white bathroom.

get malene's look

Think Color, Color, and More Color!

Malene isn't shy when it comes to color. For some new ways to bring color home, take Malene's lead and look at your floors. You can visit your local Lumber Liquidators and pick out hardwood floors in striking colors like teal and purple. When choosing the color for your walls, bring a sample of your hardwoods to the paint store and have them mix a custom color for the perfect match.

Build Shelving to Showcase Art

Build a mini gallery to showcase an ever-growing collection. Custom built-ins can be a great way to create a gallery to showcase all your favorite finds. And if built-ins aren't an option, add unique shelving to your walls to display your rotating art collection. We're a fan of IKEA "Lack" shelves. They have a modern look and can be painted to match the walls of your home for a seamless presentation.

Show Off Your Heritage

Malene loves to highlight her culture in each room of her home. You can showcase cultural items that have a special significance for you and your family through handcrafted pieces, original textiles, and pieces that remind you of your heritage. Place one or two of these items in every room for a cultural story that is carried throughout your interior.

Don't Forget the Rugs

There is no easier way to bring pattern home than through a rug or carpet. These pieces are made to sport oversize patterns in your interior. Look for high-quality rugs from vendors like Malene B, The Rug Company, ABC Carpet & Home, and antique rug vendors. Identify a pattern that's a great addition to the color palette and cultural story in your room. It can be one more statement piece in an ever-evolving space.

Pretty blocks of color are used throughout this interior. In the reading nook, blue walls and flooring are complemented by a light-blue chair and cushion. A deeper color palette is achieved with the addition of a brightly hued mixed-media piece.

We updated an Old City loft with bold patterns, original illustrations, and pieces that showcase the beauty of African American style.

JEANINE HAYS & BRYAN MASON
HOMECOMING
OLD CITY, PHILADELPHIA, PENNSYLVANIA

Everything that we can say about Philadelphia really comes down to one thing: Philly is home. And no matter where you go in life, there's always something special about coming home. After living in San Francisco for six years, we moved back home to Philadelphia and began our search for the perfect place to begin our new lives as East Coast designers and entrepreneurs.

Philadelphia is a big city with a plethora of neighborhoods. Eventually we decided that Old City would be the perfect place for our new start. It is where William Penn and the Quakers first settled, and today it's a beautiful area full of parks, amazing French-inspired and colonial architecture, a variety of boutiques, and art galleries. Best of all, the character of the buildings and homes, some of them hundreds of years old, would be a refreshing change from our California home.

Instead of looking for something especially streamlined and modern, we focused our hunt for a new place on buildings with a unique story, an interesting architectural design, and even a little bit of history.

RIGHT: We love exploring the unexpected in our neighborhood, like this cool peacock blue wall just outside our apartment building. OPPOSITE: White Moroccan poufs are a nice contrast to the vivid Sonia Delauney rug in our living room. PREVIOUS PAGE: Our living room showcases a variety of cultural influences from the African Diaspora. A salon wall features illustrations of stylish African American women, Moroccan poufs surround the coffee table, a Cameroonian Ndop cloth is our favorite throw, and AphroChic pillows bring color and pattern to the space.

We discovered a two-story loft in the center of Old City, just blocks from the Liberty Bell and the house where Betsy Ross sewed the first American flag. With its two-hundred-year history and charming interior layout, it was clear that this was the space we'd been looking for.

Smaller rooms and a railroad-style layout did not provide room for many of the larger furnishings we had purchased in San Francisco. This home's bones were more cottagey than modern, with a massive wooden fireplace, a beautiful turned-wood railing, and cozier rooms fit for smaller furnishings. Where our California white box had left everything open, this was a home where the architecture of the space would dictate the décor.

With so much character to it, we knew this would be the perfect apartment to create a true AphroChic home. We replaced our oversized modern furniture and brought in color, using bold accessories and original art to express the kind of modern, soulful style we love.

The living room was designed to be calm and relaxing. A long and comfy sectional and a sleek white-and-chrome coffee table were brought in to make it feel modern. We

layered in pattern with an amazing rug featuring a design based on the work of French artist Sonia Delaunay. The bold hues and geometric shapes the artist is known for make it a great centerpiece for the room.

We spent months sourcing the best pieces to feature on our gallery wall. Fortunately, we had been cataloging works for the "Original Art" section of the *AphroChic* blog for some time, so we had lots of great artists to choose from. We also brought in some of our favorite pieces from our last apartment. Two amazing fashion illustrations of glamorous African American women combining pencil, pen, and watercolor that we

Color, pattern, and art are an important part of the AphroChic design aesthetic. In each room in our home we introduce these elements through our vibrant textile collection and art we've collected over time.

had commissioned from Leigh Viner hang beside a third piece the artist gave to us as a gift. From Korea, friend and photographer Felicia Shelton sent us a pair of magazine covers illustrated by Stina Persson. Accentuating their beautiful figures is a mix of French, English, and Korean script that adds a typographic element to the covers, which we framed and hung. A piece from the French company Qora & Shai was also a fantastic fit. It is unquestionably one of our favorite pieces—a classic image of a sophisticated African woman.

Our fireplace mantel also called for art, and so we went to one of our favorite resources, Etsy, for some cool pieces. We came upon two great typographic pieces at the Etsy shop Urban Bazaar. As in our own designs, we love to see traditional motifs reimagined with a different cultural twist. The pieces are a modern spin on British morale posters printed during World War II sporting the now-famous motto "Keep Calm and Carry On." When we saw the slogan revised with a contemporary African American focus, we knew that we

ABOVE: A vignette of favorite pieces rests on the coffee table. **LEFT:** A carved African bust is part of a larger collection in our home, and a tangerine Anthropologie bowl features a modern ikat print.

LEFT: Sourcing African sculptures is one of Jeanine's favorite pastimes. She discovered these ebony sculptures of a mother and daughter on eBay. **OPPOSITE:** We chose typographic prints from Urban Bazaar to be the key focal points on the mantel. With one more masculine and the other decidedly feminine, they became the perfect way to express both our shared thoughts and our individual perspectives on our African American identity.

had found the right pieces for the room. On the bookshelves in our living room, nestled among all the texts on history and design, we found the perfect spots to display the global pieces we've collected through online sourcing and occasional flea market trips. Our shelves display an African fertility carving purchased during a visit to Washington, DC's Eastern Market. It's a place we visited often while Jeanine attended law school, and it was where our collection of African statues began. Eventually two African wood carvings sourced through Ebay were added to the collection right after we moved to San Francisco. And Jeanine discovered a gilded Moroccan dog statue while visiting friends on a sunny day at the Alameda Flea Market.

In the office (technically a laundry area), we realized we needed to find a way to keep the practical things like the washer, dryer, and storage accessible while also carving out the office space we sorely needed. Our solution was to hang one of our AphroChic shower curtains as a unique divider between the laundry area and the office. The playful tones of its "Brooklyn Life Outdoor" toile pattern help bring color and energy to the room while neatly dividing the space. To define the office, we brought in

CLOCKWISE: We love to collect cute accessories that set our home apart. A gold vase from Jamali Gardens is great for storing pens and pencils. A chevron rug from Gallery 51 in Philadelphia brings color and pattern into our office. And colorful AphroChic textile swatches are always on hand for reference and inspiration.

soundtrack

Tunes for a Modern Mixtape

We absolutely love to entertain, and at our parties we like to play an eclectic mix of our favorite R&B singers, pop, and some conscious rap. Here are the songs that are always in our modern, soulful style playlist:

1 "Thieves"
   —BLACKSTAR

2 "Losing You"
   —SOLANGE

3 "Beautiful Girls"
   —BOB FEAT.
   BRUNO MARS

4 "Gods"
   —MAIYSHA

5 "Love on Top"
   —BEYONCÉ

large furnishings to meet the needs of the space, and art and textiles to complete it. An antique chevron rug added color, while on the walls, a gigantic mood board helps us gather inspiration for upcoming AphroChic projects.

The office is the heart of AphroChic. Art by Bryan's father, Terry, hangs on the walls as family heirlooms. These pieces were part of a treasure trove of early works discovered in an old portfolio. We love his hatching of the clock tower at Auxerre, France, and his *House for the Tropics* looks like a perfect island getaway.

Upstairs in our bedroom loft, we wanted to bring some drama into the space, and we couldn't think of a better way to do that than by putting up our own "Haze"

wallpaper pattern to create a feature wall behind the bed. The sunny color of the updated ikat pattern greets us every morning, along with another great Etsy quote print that says, "So Many of My Smiles Begin with You." We believe that art has a place in every room, even in the bedroom, and the strong typographic piece was the perfect finishing touch for the bedroom wall.

ABOVE LEFT: We use small accessories such as vases and storage boxes to dot our space with color, This Jonathan Adler "Golden Eye" vase perfectly matches our "Haze" wallpaper. **ABOVE RIGHT:** Warm bronze sconces from Lamps Plus add a little bit of a metallic sheen to our bedroom's bright color palette. **OPPOSITE:** As textile designers, we love to layer pattern. In the bedroom, our "Haze" wallpaper creates a dramatic statement wall. Anthropologie bedding in beige, yellow, pink, and black adds a more oversize layer of pattern and a warm color palette to the room. Our "Silhouette" pillow and a Tunisian rug offer the final touches in this space.

Our bedroom has a great a mix of modern elements, classic furnishings, and bold patterns that speak to our personalities. We wanted a streamlined bed, so we went with the IKEA "Malm" bed frame to achieve the look. It's a great backdrop for the layers of pattern added by the Anthropologie bedding and the AphroChic "Silhouette" pillow that adorn it. On the floor, at the foot of the bed, is a piece that we bought while on a trip to

Paris—a Tunisian rug with a dazzling geometric design that has metallic thread woven within. We also carved out a seating area in the bedroom. A few midcentury modern pieces add a classic look.

Home is where you can be yourself, and what makes our home so comfortable is how well it expresses the blend of modern design and cultural style that we love so much. Using color, pattern, original art, and global objects, we have created a space that embraces contemporary design without losing sight of the history that shapes us or the cultures that inspire us. The relationship between the new and the traditional is the cornerstone of AphroChic, and helping others to bring new meaning to their spaces remains our ultimate goal. For us, that meant taking a line of thought that began in an anonymous white box of a house in California, and developing it into a new approach to African American design until it led us all the way home.

LEFT: A vintage chair from ReMOD Gallery in Philadelphia offers classic style in the bedroom. The shop owners provided us with the details and history of the chair, a nice benefit when you're bringing home pieces that are also collectibles. **RIGHT:** A simple typographic print from the Etsy shop Happy Deliveries makes a statement in the bedroom with a sweet sentiment.

get jeanine and bryan's look

Choose a Shade That Complements Bold Hues

When it came to choosing the color palette for our interior, we decided on a neutral beige as the main color. The color complemented the dark wood elements in our home and is a great base for many of the bright hues we brought into the interior, from purple and coral to bright yellow. Find a color that creates the perfect backdrop to your color palette. Gray, a clean white, black, and beige are all great neutral shades that you can't go wrong with.

Use Patterned Pieces to Add Color

Every patterned element that we brought into the space also brought in strong pops of color. The Sonia Delauney–inspired rug in the living room added strong geometric shapes to the room and also established the color palette of gray, purple, and coral that was repeated in our pillows and much of the artwork. A large patterned element with a variety of colors can ground your room while offering a foundation on which to build your color palette.

Create a Salon Wall

We collected a lot of art and needed to find a way to display it in a small interior. A salon wall became the perfect way to display a range of our favorite works by illustrators that we love. While the wall has various pieces from different artists, what brings everything together is the selection of black-and-white frames. We love mixing and matching IKEA "Ribba" frames for a clean look.

Bring Home Cultural Pieces from Your Travels

Whenever we travel, something has to come home with us. We've brought back wood carvings from Jamaica, paintings from Chile, and our beloved Tunisian rug from France. Each piece holds great meaning for us and represents a memory from our times abroad. Bring back items from your travels to add global style to your home.

RESOURCES

Here's our little black book on where to find inspiration and goods for modern, soulful style.

Art Museums

Art Basel Miami Beach www.miamibeach. artbasel.com. Explore the work of newcomers and cutting-edge artists from around the globe as they present their work in Miami Beach.

California African American Museum www.caamuseum.org. This museum primarily exhibits the art and culture of West Coast–based African Americans.

Charles H. Wright Museum of African American History www.thewright.org. In the heart of Detroit's cultural center, the Wright Museum houses interactive exhibits, screenings, and events that explore African American culture and history.

Diaspora Vibe www.diasporavibe.net. This Miami gallery presents must-see art by emerging artists in the Caribbean and Latin Diaspora.

Museum of Contemporary African Diaspora Arts www.mocada.org. Located in Brooklyn, MoCADA is the place to explore new mediums, editorial works, and political art that speak to the experiences of the African Diaspora.

Museum of the African Diaspora www.moadsf.org. Check out MOAD's amazing museum store that sells local and international works celebrating the African Diaspora and African American culture.

The African American Museum in Philadelphia www.aampmuseum.org. We love visiting our hometown museum's cultural exhibits on African American life in Philadelphia.

The Museum of African American Art www.maaala.org. Located in the Baldwin Hill area of Los Angeles, this museum is home to a permanent collection of works by African American artists.

The Studio Museum in Harlem www.studiomuseum.org. The place for the latest and most provocative works of African American art, the Studio Museum in Harlem has a legacy of showcasing and helping to mold great artists that we've discussed in this book, like Mickalene Thomas and Kehinde Wiley (see page 96).

Art Online

20x200 www.20x200.com. Founder Jen Bekman believes in "art for everyone." Every week new art is released, including both limited editions and affordable pieces that can be bought directly from the website.

Artaissance www.artthatfits.com. Search over three thousand prints in whatever category fits your style, from global to abstract pieces of art.

Art.com www.art.com. The ultimate art catalog. You can discover and curate your own collection, view your choices in a room setting, and easily share art that you love using social media.

Etsy www.etsy.com. An incredible resource for handmade and vintage art and home décor. You can spend hours looking for prints, paintings, and original pieces.

Gallery Hanahou www.galleryhanahou.com. Check out this online gallery's limited edition prints, fashion illustrations, fiber arts, books, and accessories.

MoMA www.momastore.org. Here you can find the best in modern and contemporary art from the most prolific artists of the twentieth and twenty-first centuries.

Society6 www.society6.com. This website is an online destination for a selection of affordable prints and framed pieces.

Artists We Love:
Where to Look for Original Pieces and Inspiration

Andrea Pippins www.ilovemyhair.com. We love Andrea's "I Love My Hair" print series, perfect for women and girls of all ages.

Andre Woolery www.andrewooleryart.com. Check out his iconic portraits, including one of Barack Obama, made with thousands of pushpins.

Cate Parr www.cateparr.com. We love her watercolors featuring beautiful women from around the globe who are soulful and striking.

Edwina Owens Elliott www.edwinaowens elliott.com. Edwina turned her love of art and design into a professional fashion illustration career, and now sells her works online.

GA Gardner www.gagardner.com. This artist creates striking cultural portraits through mixed media collages.

Jennifer Ramos www.madebygirl.com. Jen offers typographic posters and prints that are perfect for expressing yourself at home.

Kareem Iliya www.kareemiliya.com. We truly enjoy Kareem's light and ethereal fashion illustrations, many of which evoke a cultural feel.

Kehinde Wiley www.kehindewiley.com. Check out Kehinde's modern portraits of contemporary African American, African, Afro-Brazilian, Indian, Ethiopian, and Jewish men.

Lauren Bishop www.laurenbishopillustration.co.uk. This fashion illustrator offers diverse fashion illustrations, including images of Asian and Indian women.

Leigh Viner www.leighviner.com. Leigh Viner's images of modern, fashionable women are prominent in our own home.

Len Davis www.lendavis.com. Philadelphia native Len Davis creates mixed media collages using found objects, drawings, and text to develop contemporary images of African American men.

Mickalene Thomas www.mickalenethomas.com. Mickalene creates fascinating images of African American women with the use of rhinestones, acrylic, and enamel.

Qora & Shai www.qorashai-boutique.com. Looking for cool graphic art featuring a Black girl on a Vespa or with a hot pink afro? This French shop is the place to go, and they ship worldwide.

Samantha Hahn www.samanthahahn.com. Samantha is the artist behind our "Brooklyn Life" toile and "Brooklyn girl" pillows. Her fashion illustrations are among our favorites and are beautiful, soulful, and evocative.

Sonya Suhariyan www.sonyasuhariyan.com. We love Sonya's illustrations of women from around the world. Her portfolio is full of striking and diverse images for the modern illustration collector.

Stina Persson www.stinapersson.com. Stina's vibrant, edgy, and modern watercolor pieces introduced us to fashion illustration as art.

Tabitha Brown www.thepairabirds.com. Tabitha's "Yearbook" series ranks among our favorite digital illustrations. Collect over thirty of her images of distinct women and men of color.

Urban Bazaar www.etsy.com/shop/urbanbazaar. Typographic prints at Urban Bazaar turn the "Keep Calm" style of World War II into a cultural statement piece, such as "Stay Black and Remain Proud."

Yahgie www.yahgie.com. In addition to colorful textiles, this company offers bold prints that are mounted on canvas. One is featured in the home of Kalyn and Todd Chandler on page 92.

Curated Sites

1st Dibs www.1stdibs.com. Discover African art and global antiques among the fifteen-hundred-plus international antiques and vintage dealers that sell through this site.

55 Downing Street www.55downingstreet.com. Started by the founder of Lamps Plus, 55 Downing Street is the place to go for contemporary furnishings at a great price.

Fab www.fab.com. On Fab you can find deals on distinctive furniture, original art, and very cool accessories.

Gilt www.gilt.com. Be on the lookout for Turkish towels, dhurries, ikat textiles, and vintage products on this site.

Joss & Main www.jossandmain.com. Joss & Main offers everything from colorful tableware to home furnishing collections inspired by global destinations.

Keep www.keep.com. A shopable Pinterest-style site, Keep lets you choose the home décor you love and shop for it directly from the website.

MyHabit www.myhabit.com. At MyHabit you will find trendy items featuring ikat, suzani, and chevron prints.

One Kings Lane www.onekingslane.com. Check out this curated site's themed sales on things like mixing and matching prints.

Rue La La www.ruelala.com. This site's *Style Guide* blog provides great tips from bloggers and editors on how to decorate your home with style.

The Foundary www.thefoundary.com. Check out this specialty shop for home and style filled with affordable items for any room in your home.

Global Objects

ABC Carpet & Home www.abchome.com. ABC Carpet & Home is our go-to place in New York for everything cultural and global in design. Explore furniture and accessories from South Africa, Morocco, India, and South America in just a few steps.

Anthropologie www.anthropologie.com. You can discover beautiful furnishings featuring global-inspired designs, from upholstered chairs in suzani prints to settees covered in African wax prints.

AphroChic www.aphrochic.com. Our textiles blend modern design with an African American aesthetic including Kuba, ikat, chevron, and afro pillows, table linens, and organic shower curtains.

BELDI www.shopbeldi.com. Visit Beldi for handcrafted pieces from Morocco, such as candy-colored poufs, handblown glassware, ceramics, and a rich collection of boucherouite rugs.

Calypso St. Barth www.calypsostbarth.com. This Manhattan brick-and-mortar store and online shop is filled with beautiful furniture, pillows, and bedding inspired by ancient cultures.

Dar Leone www.dar-leone.com. A destination for African Kuba cloth pillows, ikat and chevron textiles, and Senegalese baskets.

Faded Empire www.fadedempire.com. Visit this shop for a colorful collection of vintage kantha quilts and Turkish kilims.

Hammocks & High Tea www.hammocks andhightea.com. Our friend Karen Young in Brooklyn creates culturally inspired pillows influenced by Turkish, Maasai, and Moroccan cultures.

John Derian www.johnderian.com. Visit this shop for Moroccan wares, including wedding blankets, poufs, and vintage trays.

John Robshaw www.johnrobshaw.com. Explore the store's specialized souk full of Indian block prints and vintage pieces, including suzani throws and pillows, dhurries, batik, and kantha pillows.

Layla www.layla-bklyn.com. Next time you're in Brooklyn, visit Layla for its well-curated collection of global textiles, including hand-blocked bedding and traditional Indian towels.

L'aviva Home www.lavivahome.com. Laura Aviva, former creative director of *Travel + Leisure* magazine, has curated a collection of handmade textiles from artisans in Uzbekistan, Kyrgyzstan, Bolivia, Egypt, Cameroon, and more.

Le Marche St. George www.marchestgeorge .com. This online shop has a colorful collection of embroidered Otomí pillows handcrafted in Mexico.

Lotus Bleu www.lotusbleudesign.com. Textile heaven right in San Francisco with an eclectic mix of pillows, table linens, rugs, and wallpaper all featuring cultural motifs with a modern twist.

Le Souk www.soukshop.com. Le Souk offers a great mix of global furnishings, such as Moroccan tea tables, Senegalese stools, and Egyptian pendants.

Madeline Weinrib www.madelineweinrib .com. A great source for many cultural designs, such as classic dhurries, hand-knotted Tibetan carpets, vintage Moroccan rugs, and ikat, suzani, and Indian block-print pillows and fabrics.

Mercantile www.scoutdesignsmercantile.big cartel.com. A shop offering one-of-a-kind vintage pieces, including Cameroonian juju hats, antique Persian rugs, and furnishings from India and beyond.

Object Interiors www.oistudio.com. Founded by BOA, whose home is featured in Part II of this book, OI offers eco-friendly, contemporary furniture inspired by nature and international travels.

Pearl River www.pearlriver.com. Home to Asian ceramics, lanterns, Chinese garden stools, and Buddhist statues, Pearl River is a trove of Asian-inspired design.

Red Thread Souk www.redthreadsouk.com. Fellow blogger Maryam Montague from *My Marrakesh* has opened her very own shop with vintage treasures from Morocco, especially Moroccan boucherouite and Beni Ourain carpets and wedding blankets.

Rummage www.rummagehome.com. Interior designer Kishani Perera's shop brings together an eclectic mix of pieces, both old and new.

Serena & Lily www.serenaandlily.com. This company's furnishings and accessories include colorful Senegalese baskets, striped Turkish bath towels, pearl inlaid furnishings, and poufs in a variety of hues.

Sheherazade www.sheherazadehome.com. We love this shop for its unique upholstered seating, including kantha-upholstered settees and ikat-upholstered lounge chairs.

Tazi www.tazidesigns.com. This shop has a vast collection of Moroccan, Islamic, and Moorish décor, from tea glasses to mosaic tables and large antique doors.

The South is Blooming www.thesouthis blooming.com. This shop offers a beautiful array of African items via the Netherlands, including South African cushions, handcrafted bowls, and beautiful linens.

Modern Furniture & Accessories

BoConcept www.boconcept.com. Danish design for the urban dweller, BoConcept offers streamlined sofas, chairs, and storage that fits beautifully into urban spaces.

Blu Dot www.bludot.com. Home to innovative furnishings, Blu Dot stocks colorful dining room tables, seating, beds, and sofas.

Bungalow 5 www.bungalow5.com. Coffee tables, side tables, consoles, lighting—it can all be found at Bungalow 5 in beautiful silhouettes and stunning lacquer finishes.

Busybee Homestore and Design Center www.busybeephilly.com. One of Philadelphia's most modern home décor stores, Busybee carries everything from furniture to lighting, pillows, and interior design services.

Design Within Reach www.dwr.com. The home of modern classics like the Cherner Chair, Ghost Chair, and Saarinen Tulip Table, DWR is a must-visit for the modern furniture aficionado.

DwellStudio www.dwellstudio.com. Modern patterns are the foundation of DwellStudio style. Check out its ever-expanding collection of furniture, décor, children's accessories, and textiles.

Iannone Design www.iannonedesign.com. Store your clothing in style with eco-friendly furniture designs that include sideboards in bold floral patterns, graphic armoires, and laser-cut filing cabinets with cool designs.

Jonathan Adler www.jonathanadler.com. The store for print, pattern, bold colors, and happy chic. Check out Adler's line of colorful pottery, luxe patterned seating, and updated midcentury modern classics.

Kartell www.kartell.com. Look for iconic pieces like the Bourgie Table Lamp and new lines from artists such as Lenny Kravitz.

Knoll www.knoll.com. This Pennsylvania brand has a long history and is still producing beautiful modern pieces like the Barcelona Chair, Bertoia Lounge Seating, and the Womb Chair.

ReMOD Gallery www.remodgallery.com. Literally our next door neighbor, owner Amber Skymer knows how to curate midcentury modern design so that it looks brand-new.

Room & Board www.roomandboard.com. This modern showroom sells midcentury modern classics by Ray and Charles Eames and Herman Miller, new American-made furniture, cozy rugs, and wall art.

Shop Ten 25 www.shopten25.com. Modern, eclectic, and chic items are all available in this online boutique curated by interior designer Abbe Fenimore.

Tabletop DC www.tabletopdc.com. Whenever we visit DC, a trip to Tabletop is always on the agenda. It is the go-to place for modern accessories, art, furniture, and one-of-a-kind pieces.

West Elm www.westelm.com. We're a fan of the store's designer collaborations, which include limited-edition pieces from artists and modern and international designers.

Rugs & Flooring

ABC Carpet www.abccarpet.com. The number one place to shop for cultural rugs. The store's Color Reform collection is stunning, featuring a vast collection of over-dyed rugs in bold hues.

Angela Adams www.angelaadams.com. This Maine designer creates bold designs filled with lots of color and texture that are perfect for laying down a unique color and pattern story at home.

Anthropologie www.anthropologie.com. One of our favorite places to shop for culturally inspired rugs. At Anthro you can find everything from modern dhurries, kilims, berbers, and boucherouite rugs.

Domestic Modern www.domesticmodern .com. One of the easiest sites to find the perfect rug. You can search for modern designs and unique prints, and even refine your search by color.

FLOR www.flor.com. The ultimate destination for flooring, this site allows you to mix and match FLOR carpet tiles to create your own custom rug or carpet.

Gallery 51 www.gallery51.net. This Philadelphia store is home to antique rugs and rare textiles from around the globe, including antique kilims, Oriental rugs, kente cloth, Cameroon Ndop cloth, and Kuba cloth.

Malene B www.maleneb.com. Find custom carpets featuring batik prints, designs featuring the dress of the Wolof people of Senegal, colorful rugs inspired by Haitian culture, and hand-tufted carpets. Malene's home is featured in Part II of this book.

Morris Etc. www.morrisetc.com. Brooklynites Amy and Brett Morris have brought Peruvian design to the states with a collection of handmade rugs in trendy shades and striped patterns.

Popham Design www.pophamdesign.com. Explore a whole range of cement tiles, including the traditional Moroccan lantern, Zulu, and Asian-inspired designs, and cool geometric shapes in soft and elegant colors.

The Rug Company www.therugcompany .com. This is the place for unique statement rugs designed by top designers, including Diane von Fürstenberg, Jonathan Adler, Kelly Wearstler, Martyn Lawrence-Bullard, and more.

Wallpaper

AphroChic www.aphrochicshop.com. Choose from our hand-screened or eco-friendly digitally printed wallpaper with African American, Kuba, chevron, ikat, and Cameroonian-inspired designs.

Cole & Son www.cole-and-son.com. One of the most beautiful collections of luxury wallpapers, from colorful patterns by Vivienne Westwood to contemporary designs by Fornasetti.

Ferm Living www.ferm-living.com. Geometric prints, oversized florals, and cutting-edge colors make these designs fresh and modern.

Given Campbell www.givencampbell.com. We first spotted Given's work in *Domino* magazine years ago. Her wallpaper offers a great graphic punch in plenty of fun shades to enjoy at home.

Graham & Brown www.grahambrown.com. Offering some of the most innovative wallpaper lines, including our own, Graham & Brown is the best place to go for stylish designer wallpapers.

Hygge & West www.hyggeandwest.com. Hygge & West offers a curated collection of artsy wallpaper patterns from indie designers Joy Cho, Julia Rothman, Terrence Payne, Emily Isabella, and Pattern People.

Kreme www.kremelife.com. Kreme wallpaper designs are vibrant, sophisticated, and California cool. We especially love the Muse Collection featuring watercolor and digitally printed papers.

MIO www.mioculture.com. You can create your very own wallpaper pattern using MIO's 3D wallpaper tiles.

WallArt www.mywallart.com. A multitude of 3D wallpaper designs. Panels can be hung and easily painted in your favorite shade.

Design Inspiration

Anthology www.anthologymag.com. This magazine, sold in Anthropologie stores, features real homes with natural, soulful style.

Apartment Therapy www.apartmenttherapy .com. Check out the daily house tours, DIY projects, before-and-afters, and budget finds from real apartment dwellers.

Better Homes and Gardens www.bhg.com. We love the magazine's style blog, which is filled with fresh approaches for updating your interior.

Elle Decor www.elledecor.com. A fantastic site that features an expansive gallery of interiors and expanded content from the magazine.

HGTV www.hgtv.com. Home galleries, color features, and articles on home décor all serve as design inspiration on this website.

Homesessive www.homesessive.com. This home design site is full of budget-friendly ideas, DIY projects, and outdoor decorating projects.

House Beautiful www.housebeautiful.com. We really love the decorating and design ideas, especially the color tips and resources.

Houzz www.houzz.com. Browse idea books by style and look for cultural and modern spaces.

Lonny Magazine www.lonnymag.com. This home décor e-mag cofounded by our photographer, Patrick Cline, makes you want to pin your beautiful images for your mood boards.

Matchbook Magazine www.matchbookmag .com. Cofounders Katie Armour and Jane Lily Warren call it their "field guide to a charmed life," and we could not agree more.

Pantone www.pantone.com. The international resource on color trends that will help you identify the best shades for your home.

Pinterest www.pinterest.com. The website for creating visual mood boards of your favorite finds from around the web.

Rue www.ruemag.com. Glamorous interiors, color and pattern inspiration, and great home and city tours make this one that we bookmark.

ACKNOWLEDGMENTS

There are so many people whose hard work and belief in this project helped make this book a reality. From the very beginning, AphroChic has been a family affair. And so our first thanks go to our sister Angela Belt and our brother-in-law Leon Belt. You two have been with us from the start of the blog to our first steps as a textile company, and now on this wonderful adventure to write our first book. Your amazing talents in so many different areas have brought every one of our projects to another level, and yet with this book you somehow managed to top everything that you have done before. We cannot thank you enough for your hard work and continued support.

We would also like to thank our friend and photographer Patrick Cline, who is responsible for the incredible photos that bring this book to life. Another longtime member of the AphroChic family, Patrick captured our vision for the brand in our very first AphroChic product shoot, and we were thrilled to have him on our team as we tackled our most ambitious project to date. Patrick, you are without doubt the fastest, most skilled, and pound-for-pound most fun photographer we have ever worked with. Your photographs are nothing short of spectacular and we just can't thank you enough.

To Brittany Ambridge, the newest addition to the AphroChic family, thank you for keeping everything moving smoothly during our shoots. More important, you kept everyone laughing so much that the days just flew by. We can't think of a better team than you and Patrick. You're two of our favorite people to hang out with, and you were exactly what this book needed. We can't wait to do it again and again.

We would also like to extend a huge thank-you to our book team at Clarkson Potter for bringing this whole project together: Pam Krauss, Doris Cooper, Jane Treuhaft, Angelin Borsics, Ashley Tucker, Alexis Mentor, Terry Deal, Carly Gorga, Sean Boyles, and Mary Anne Stewart. Special thanks go to our editor, Angelin Borsics, for believing in the unique voice of our brand. Angelin, you helped us create a finished product that we can all be very proud of. You were encouraging, inquisitive, understanding, and above all you pushed us to present our ideas in the best possible way. We're so happy to have had this experience with you.

A big thank-you to Rich Pedine, our friend and publicist and one of AphroChic's biggest cheerleaders. Rich, you don't know how many of your ideas we've gone through with just so we can look at each other and say, "Well, Rich seems to like it." You make us laugh, you keep us on target, and you make us look good. We couldn't ask for more.

And extra-special thanks to our friend Danielle Colding. We are so honored to have you write the foreword for this book. There is no other designer who truly understands the importance of AphroChic's message and our focus on cultural style like you do. Thank you.

In addition to our main team, we received immeasurable help on a number of shoots from our assistant stylists Sierra Baskind, Tina Karkera, and Kalyan Anamula. Special thanks also to little Priyanka Anamula for being so good to her mom while she was helping us out. A special shout-out as well to Dr. Boogie for bringing Hollywood-level styling to our Venice, California, shoot.

There were more than a few companies that very generously donated their products so that we could show you what's truly special about AphroChic style. In particular we would like to thank ABC Carpet & Home, Anthropologie, John Robshaw, and Room & Board for lending so many beautiful pieces. We owe an especially big thank-you to Jonathan Adler. Whether we were in Philly, Brooklyn, or LA, we always knew that we could count on the good people at JA to have exactly what we needed. Thank you to our Old City neighbors Amber Skymer from ReMOD Gallery and Craig Williams from Gallery 51. Craig, your inspiring level of knowledge on global rugs both ancient and contemporary and your willingness to donate your pieces and time helped us make a much stronger book. Thank you to Nissan for making the LA trip one of the highlights of the entire book experience and providing us with a vehicle while we were there (that car is now the next big item on our wish list!).

Of course, this book could never have been done without the kind and patient indulgence of the homeowners and designers who contributed their time and space to making it happen. So to Anna Powers and Mark Miklosovich, BOA and Tara Bethea, Chad Thomas, Emily Henderson, James Saavedra, Joy Simpson, Kalyn and Todd Chandler, Maiysha Simpson, Malene Barnett, Matthew Lanphier, Nicole Cohen, Nikita Adams, the Bowmans, and Vanessa De Vargas, thank you for inviting us into your homes and sharing your designs and your lives with us for a day. Each of you has turned your home into an amazing statement of who you are. We are extremely grateful to have had the opportunity to share your accomplishments with the world.

Finally we'd like to show our appreciation to our moms Debra Hays and Jacquelyn Mason, our dads Terry Mason and Charles Hays, and our sister and brother Lesli Harper and Andre O'Brien for all of the love and support that it takes to make two people believe that they can do something like this. And to all of our readers, customers, supporters, followers, and fans, thank you for taking this journey with us.

INDEX

Note: Page numbers in *italics* include references to photo captions. For page ranges, one page in *italics* indicates at least one reference to photo a caption.